SURPRISED
BY
TRAGEDY

TIM COX

SURPRISED BY TRAGEDY
Copyright ©2018 by Tim Cox

ISBN: 9781732411807

Published by TMC Press

DEDICATION

To my amazing wife, Diane.

Contents

INTRODUCTION

You probably just did it...and now you're doing it again as you wonder what I am talking about.

The average person inhales and exhales about 20,000 times a day, and each one of them is important. If you are healthy, breathing is so effortless and natural that you take it for granted. Yet if it were difficult, and the next breath hard to come by, it would probably affect all your priorities. It certainly did for me.

On my 58th birthday, as my family stood around me singing, it took me several breaths to blow out the five or six candles on my cake. Even more disturbing, I was told by doctors that without a transplant, my days on this earth were going to be far less than I had planned.

Please understand, this is not a book about how to survive a double lung transplant. Only a small percentage of men and women will ever have to address such a life or death situation.

Rather, I am asking you to join me on a journey that answers these and many other questions:

- How do you respond when your hopes and dreams are put on hold?
- What happens to your confidence when you can no longer fit the pieces of your life's puzzle together?
- Why is it easier to help others instead of helping yourself?
- What steps should you take to prepare for a crisis?
- What is it like to be totally dependent on family, friends, and physicians?
- Where is your faith when you survive a dangerous operation only to become the victim of a stroke?
- How to wrestle with the "Why me?" questions.

- What are the most valuable lessons to be learned from a tragedy?
- Why is it important to form a "crisis-ready" team?

I don't know the circumstances you or someone you love may be facing. It may involve health, finances, relationships, or a host of other challenges. My desire is that if you are *Surprised by Tragedy*, these words will give you strength, courage, and hope.

– Tim Cox

1

RUNNING ON EMPTY

Springtime in the Carolinas is absolutely gorgeous. Birds chirping, trees budding, azaleas in full bloom—and those picture-perfect, deep blue skies.

As a native of the Great Lakes state, Michigan, I actually looked forward to cranking up my lawn mower and enjoying the fresh air, while my friends up north might still be shoveling snow.

For me, however, the spring of 2014 was different. By late March, I told my wife, Diane, "Honey, I don't understand what's going on, but I think we need to buy a self-propelled mower."

"Why?" she wanted to know.

"After a few minutes of mowing I feel like I'm out of breath."

It was really getting to me. I'd literally have to sit down and rest four or five times before finishing the job. If you knew the size of my yard, you would realize how embarrassing that was for me.

Was it the humidity? My limited exercise routine? But at the age of 56, my lawn appeared bigger, the gentle slope of my yard felt like a hill, and the grass seemed to be growing thicker and faster.

Whatever the reason, I began to enlist friends, family, and eventually the services of a landscape company to tackle the yard work.

I didn't understand my breathing problem. As a pastoral staff member at a local church in Charlotte, my work was emotionally taxing but certainly wasn't physically strenuous. I was constantly running out of breath; and even when sitting down I would have an aggravatingly constant cough.

Diane suggested, "I think you'd better make an appointment with our doctor"—which I did.

At the clinic, they said, "Mr. Cox, we need to schedule a stress test."

When the results came in, the doctor told me, "We don't see anything suspicious in all the normal places, but since your breathing problem is not getting any better, I have ordered some additional tests."

He added, "We want to take a closer look at the right ventricle, which leads to the lungs."

The blood work, x-rays, and additional stress test began immediately, culminating with a lung biopsy.

At one of the earlier appointments, the doctor stated, "I believe you have some form of pulmonary fibrosis, but there are many different types. There is one really bad type. Let's hope we can avoid that one."

AN UNEXPECTED MEDICAL EDUCATION

A team of specialists was assigned to my case, and on July 3, 2014, my wife and I were asked to come to the appointment that would have conclusive results. There, I was informed, "Mr. Cox, you have the bad one. It's called Idiopathic Pulmonary Fibrosis (IPF)."

After a few minutes of back-and-forth questioning he told me, "Unfortunately, your biopsies confirmed that you have the most serious form of the disease."

I asked, "How serious?"

The doctor's answer was chilling: "Almost half of those with this diagnosis die within two to three years. There is currently no treatment. The only cure is a lung transplant."

With each statement he made I felt a combination of fears, yet increasing focus, wanting to know more. Every labored breath became more precious and my mind raced ahead in disbelief.

I learned that Pulmonary Fibrosis is usually identified as an autoimmune disease, which means that some "trigger" may have told my cells to attack my lungs and work to destroy the millions of air sacs that are needed to distribute oxygen to the rest of my body. My form of the disease would lead to complete scarring in both my lungs, and at some point in the future I would be unable to take my next breath.

The word "Idiopathic" intrigued me. I found out it meant—of no known origin. But it caused me to wonder, *How could I have contracted such a disease?*

Let's see. I'd never been a coal miner, or a farmer working around large amounts of pesticides. Well, I did scrape my tile floor a few years earlier as we renovated, and there may have been some asbestos fibers. Could it have happened on that mission trip to the Ukraine when I was 100 miles downwind four years after the Chernobyl nuclear accident? I tried to imagine every possible scenario of my recent and distant past.

It didn't matter. I had the disease and, at the time, there was no approved treatment to hopefully deter its progress.

I was informed that my only option was to stay healthy long enough to go through the qualifying process for a lung transplant.

My understanding of the problem was limited, but we had done enough research to discover that there had been some cases of remission—which offered a glimmer of hope.

LOOKING BACK

One thing was for certain. I was thankful to be living in a time where organ transplants were possible, and had an increasing rate of success.

During the mid-20th century there had been hundreds of failed experiments with heart and lung transplants on animals.

The first human lung transplantation was performed on June 11, 1963, at the University Hospital in Jackson, Mississippi, by surgeon James D. Hardy and his team. The patient, identified later as 58-year-old convicted murderer John Richard Russell, survived for 18 days. He developed progressive kidney failure and became increasingly malnourished. He was started on peritoneal dialysis but died due to renal failure.

Headlines were also being made on the heart front when the first human-to-human heart transplant was performed in Cape Town by South African cardiac surgeon Christiaan Barnard. The recipient, 54-year-old Louis Washkansky, regained full consciousness and lived for just over two weeks before he passed away from pneumonia—the suppression of his immune system by the anti-rejection drugs being a major contributing factor.

In the 1960s and 1970s, multiple attempts at lung transplantation failed because of rejection and problems with bronchial healing. It was only after the invention of the heart-lung machine, coupled with the development of effective drugs, that organs such as the lungs could be transplanted with a reasonable chance of patient recovery.

The statistics and stories are sobering. My journey was just beginning, but I would benefit from the lessons learned of every lung transplant ever performed.

THE ROAD AHEAD

Regarding my diagnosis, Diane began pursuing every nutritional advantage that might be gained through food choices. My attention, however, was centered on one goal: *Where do you go when you need a lung transplant?*

I knew it was going to be a long, arduous journey that would have its ups and downs on a daily, even hourly basis. It was all because my body had been tricked to attack itself—and I was well aware that I needed help I could not personally provide.

As the truth sank in, the tears and fears spilled over. Conversations the rest of the day, especially with our children, were difficult, but determined. We thought we had strong faith, but was it strong enough for something like this?

"LET'S GO!"

Suddenly, all my hopes and dreams for the future were placed on hold. Before the diagnosis, I had expectations for a life that had me holding hands with Diane in one of those comfortable Southern rocking chairs for 30 years or more. But when you are told you might only live two or three years without a transplant, that changes everything. But does it?

None of us have been promised that we will get out of this life alive. Yet, I had just been given the possibility of a rather clear "deadline," which caused me to evaluate, focus, and repurpose the priorities of each day. There would be new things to learn and to start doing with passion, and there would be some activities that I'd have to slow down on or stop completely.

However, my core commitment was as clear to me as ever—*to love God and others with a desire to encourage the next growth step either **to** or **with** Jesus.*

So I turned to Diane and uttered two words: "Let's go!"

By that I meant that I have the gift of today, so

we should prepare for anything.

The phrase is often used in the sports world as a rally cry encouraging the team to even greater achievement. Coaches and players alike shout the challenge. Sometimes it is whispered as the motivating phrase that solidifies the focus and determination of one player.

No matter the obstacle, "Let's go!" signals the commitment to give our best to the task ahead.

Being totally transparent, I used the phrase to combat discouragement. Especially during those first few confusing days when it felt overwhelming to look ahead in light of all that needed to happen.

As my mind raced and my emotions spun from all the reality crashing in around me, I was surprised how I wanted to withdraw and retreat. At the same time I had a strong desire to be with my family and friends.

In my younger years I was encouraged to be more of an enthusiastic "ready, fire, aim" type of guy. Initially that made little sense to me coming from a childhood of hunting with my dad. To have a successful hunt had far more to do with the preparations and careful aim than squeezing the trigger. However, time had taught me that I can overanalyze and prepare to the point that an opportunity is missed. There comes a moment when action must be taken with confidence even though all the answers are not known.

Every day I faced decisions that needed solutions, yet all the information I found left me unsatisfied. I did discover that there is a lot of uncertainty about even being placed on the lung transplant list and qualifying for new lungs.

LOSING CONTROL

You've probably heard the phrase, "It has to get worse before it gets better."

That was an apt description of my situation. Although I was still in the process of exploring several transplant centers, a physician's assistant had advised me of this possibility: "Your fibrosis may have been discovered in the early stages, and might progress very slowly. If so, that means there could be years of waiting for your lungs to decline. I suggest you try to stay healthy in every other way."

The exact stage of my illness was still being determined because certain test results showed how little I needed to supplement my breathing with extra oxygen.

Earlier, during our July 3 appointment, the doctor told us that The Cleveland Clinic in Ohio was one of the best transplant centers in the country. During our research we looked at the many different options we would have to pursue to being accepted as a candidate at this world-renowned hospital.

Finally, I was informed, "Within a couple of months, the Transplant Center will call you in for several days of testing to determine exactly how soon you might be on the candidate list, and how high your number will be."

I had heard of some candidates who waited for several years because their lungs declined so slowly. Waiting to get "sick enough" brought many questions to my mind, but they all fell in the category of "how close to the edge of the cliff would I be expected to walk?"

My personality is wired to strategize and plan so that risks are minimized. I want to decide what happens, and when. Like most people, I prefer to be in charge.

Practically speaking, I put lots of things in the faith category when in reality I try to hold power over how much faith is to be exercised. I say, "God is leading," but in many decisions, if things are not going the way I want, I consider how to take back the reins of my life. I am still trying to learn to totally trust God.

Yes, I was losing control, but that was not a bad thing, because it was causing my faith to strengthen and grow.

As I kept learning what faith in God looks like for a new set of lungs, I smiled when I figured that the greeting card industry was missing an opportunity for a new line of get well cards. The message needs to convey "Best wishes for continued great health in all ways, while your lungs predictably decline!"

A SIGH OF RELIEF

There were many hoops to jump through during the process of being approved as a candidate at a lung transplant center—primarily dictated by what is covered by insurance companies. Even though they were close to home, the transplant centers connected to the University of North Carolina and Duke University would not be handling my procedure.

So in late July, several weeks after my diagnosis, we decided that my case would be in the hands of The Cleveland Clinic in Ohio. We were cautiously excited...and nervous and scared...but committed to go, especially since they had performed more than 1,100 lung transplants with long term survival rates above the national average.

They immediately scheduled me for tests and evaluations to determine my priority, and to discover information that would guide them in the future to a possible donor match.

I had no way of knowing what trying times my wife and I had ahead of us. The unique combination of pain, optimism, and confusion clouded every day and made sleeping at night difficult. Yet, if I had known then what I know now about my future, I would have still done what happened next.

I took Diane's hand and whispered, "Let's go!"

2

THE NEW NORMAL

In Charlotte, my wife worked in the investment industry and one of her responsibilities was to create a welcoming environment for those who came to meet with a financial advisor.

In 2014, a few days after my initial diagnosis, a first-time client entered the office for an appointment. As Diane greeted her and became further engaged in conversation, she asked, "What brought you to Charlotte?"

She learned that a few years earlier, the woman had followed her daughter and family to the area so she could be near her grandkids.

As the conversation continued, Diane was told

that the daughter had recently moved to accept a position as a key director at, of all places, The Cleveland Clinic of Ohio.

This seemed more than mere coincidence. As my wife shared my need for a lung transplant, this "stranger" offered insight and encouragement on why The Cleveland Clinic needed to be our choice. She even called her daughter the same day, who also passed along very helpful counsel and advice.

Later, Diane and this woman both agreed: "God works in mysterious ways!"

AN UNEXPECTED PRAYER

As we prepared to head to Cleveland and begin the evaluations at what was to be our transplant center, everything moved to another level of reality. Reading about the process ahead, I continued to have many more questions than answers. There was so little I knew about the future. As a pastor I am constantly called on to pray for others, but I found it difficult to pray for myself.

However, it was heartening and humbling to hear that so many were talking to the Lord on my behalf.

One of our daughter's friends typed out her prayer for me and passed it along. As I was about to enter a new stage of my life, it really touched me:

God, I praise you because You go before us. I praise You because You fight for our good in all things. I praise You because You are for us so who can be against us. I praise You that You hear the cries of our heart and that Your Spirit intercedes when we don't have the words to say in prayer to You.

I praise You that we can cast all our anxiety on You because You care for us. I thank You for Your presence in Melissa's family's lives and their desire that You be glorified in their struggle.

Father, I pray overall that Your blanket of peace may overcome them as a whole. I pray that when doubt creeps in their minds that they might combat it with the sword of Your Word. I pray that You would surround them with people who might speak Your truth when they do not have the strength.

As Melissa's dad and family endure the struggle of waiting, I pray that they would feel You waiting with them. I pray that this time unites her parents as they both seek You and

Your will in the tough times.

Lord, You said that You wanted us to have life and have it to the full. Please let this time of waiting still involve full life.

We trust You and Your will. We love You and know You know what's best. Thank You that we are not in charge and help us to fully rely on You.

In Your name I pray...Amen.

THE EVALUATION

My appointment at The Cleveland Clinic was scheduled for mid-August and we packed up for the journey. However, we had no idea whether this would be a short trip or an extended adventure. I was introduced to many of the tests that I continue to this day. How much of my life would be put on "hold"?

Without question, Diane and I both felt that the care and attentiveness of The Clinic staff was exceptional. However, after several days of tests and consultations, my body was sore and I was extremely tired.

After the medical team and staff evaluated all my

records, I was told, "Mr. Cox, you are too healthy to be on the transplant list at this time."

They considered me to be an excellent candidate because of the support structure and overall health history. My lungs were an average size and my blood type was not rare. The disease itself was in both of my lower lungs. So they said, "You will be monitored in order to watch for progression of the fibrosis."

They added that unless my condition drastically changed, my next appointment in Cleveland would be several months down the road—which meant more waiting.

My wife and I both received notebooks full of information for the patient and the caregiver. Everything was orchestrated to be both an introduction and detailed overview of my condition and the path ahead. We were encouraged to stay in close touch by phone or email, and to have a long distance relationship that would allow them to respond to all of our needs.

A NEW ROUTINE

Back home in Charlotte, there were many changes to my everyday routine. Here is what my "new normal" looked like.

29

First: Parking was easier.

My handicapped parking pass arrived in the mail, so my walks into offices and stores became shorter. This was definitely a huge help and almost made me want to shop more! I did have to endure a few "what's-wrong-with-you?" looks, but I knew that would change when I was on oxygen.

Second: Pulmonary Rehab three days a week.

It was helpful to have a planned workout program under the monitoring of respiratory therapists. I was on supplemental oxygen the whole time to keep my saturation levels in the right range during the exertion. The conditioning helped to keep my overall health as strong as possible for the present, and for the eventual transplant.

I was told by the longtime members of that rehab group, many with COPD or other lung diseases, that I was now part of the "Wheezers." When they found out I was a pastor, they immediately "voted" me chaplain of the group.

Third: New friendships.

I was introduced to a gentleman named David, who became a source of tremendous encouragement. He lived with the same type of pulmonary fibrosis for years after his biopsy as the disease progressed through his lungs

In the fall of 2013 he went through a successful double lung transplant that led to a strong recovery. David's guidance reminded me of a five-day back-packing "hike" I had taken in the Grand Canyon with a group several years earlier. We trekked over some of the most stunning ribbons of trails in nature. The canyon has a magnificence and grandeur that is impossible to fully describe through words.

In order to create a healthy respect for the dangers of hiking the canyon, the Park Service has posted many strong warnings to discourage casual day hikers. Even as you stand at some of the trailheads with your bottle of water, lathered in sunscreen, signs state eye-opening facts and stories about people who have died doing exactly what you are thinking of doing. It is such a stark contrast to the fun of all the breezy overlooks offering spectac-ular vistas to tourists enjoying the souvenirs and snacks in the many gift shops. The difference for us was that we had a guide who had led many groups before ours.

Everything in our 55lb backpacks had a purpose. We were briefed several times on what to prepare for and how we would face expected challenges. Even with all these preparations, those five days and nights brought many surprises and dangers that had each of us questioning what we had gotten ourselves into. Our guide was an invaluable resource who kept us focused and made the trip an unforgettable experience.

Facing the realities of decreasing lung capacity and the expected future of a transplant surgery I was thankful for the incredible team of friends who helped make the adventure much easier.

I was especially grateful for David, who helped prepare me for my upcoming pulmonary "grand canyon" experience. He had struggled with the same disease I faced and two years earlier had a double lung transplant. He calls it his "second wind" and he was continuing to do extremely well. Although we both knew that no two journeys with this disease and surgery are exactly the same, David became my "go-to guide" when I wanted to better understand or discuss any current reality or imagine a future possibility. The key to any guide's answers and advice is that they have an understanding because of having faced the same or very similar challenge. A good mentor gives clarity, perspective, encouragement, correction, and sometimes just listens.

I have often challenged parents and couples to have certain friends who are five years ahead of their parenting stage or marriage journey. It is also helpful to be around experienced individuals when facing a tough health situation with many new realities.

IT WAS MY TURN

I have always enjoyed watching people, engaging with them, and experiencing things together. I love hearing stories of how individuals met, places they have traveled, and funny things that have happened along the way. We were not made to be constantly alone but to enjoy the sharpening and strengthening effect from being with others—men and women with whom you can both give and receive—who you trust and who trust you. That is the beauty of being "in community."

You never realize how badly you need others until life throws you a curve and gets really tough—when you are hurting or facing a crisis; the problem is compounded in the aloneness you feel. You long to hear someone else's voice and experience their presence, or just to receive a thoughtful card. These expressions of kindness often soothe the fear and encourage strength. The comfort of a loving circle of friends is invaluable.

For years I have had the privilege of serving with a community of faith who places a high value on "struggling well with life." As pastor of families I did my best to live out that mission while focusing on relationships. I felt comfortable celebrating milestones, sharing child-raising stories, or counseling those in deep pain.

Now it was my turn. I was heading down a trail that even the most optimistic in the medical profession agreed would be long and difficult. Yet I knew just enough information to see the next step or two of the journey before more foggy questions swirled around in my head, bringing raindrops of doubt.

When the sun breaks through, it is usually escorted by the quiet and simple love expressions of a friend or family member.

THE REAL BATTLE

Our son Steve researched the new drugs and treatments that were being developed for slowing the scarring of fibrosis in the lungs. He found research and studies reporting new medical developments in the treatment of donor lungs that showed promise for increasing the survival rates.

It was at this time the Federal Drug Administration approved two drugs for treatment of patients with IPF in the United States. My doctor prescribed OFEV, and I began taking the pills and dealing with the digestive side effects. We all hoped it would slow down the scarring in my lungs.

Even with my family's support, I discovered that my hardest battle was mostly mental. I tried to be thankful, positive, and intentional every day while planning for a decline in energy, activity, and health.

I was reminded of an important truth that helps, partly because of it's simplicity. A friend who also lives with a chronic illness stated, "Today is the best day I have." He added, "Sure, I plan, exercise, and prepare for the future. However, I do all that in the gift of today."

I am a firm believer that mental and spiritual health are the foundation of physical health.

THE CIRCUMSTANCES HAD CHANGED

To be honest, I was enjoying this interval of several weeks without a doctor visit or being stuck with a needle. Pardon the pun, but those weeks were definitely "a breath of fresh air."

I thought my pulmonary rehab workouts and new routine while living with the disease would be fairly easy, but I was wrong.

I soon realized that I couldn't walk fast for long periods unless I was connected to supplemental oxygen—so that crimped my plans. In fact my walks became strolls, and even then I had to stop to catch my breath if there was any incline whatsoever. Since I knew that I would eventually be on this form of oxygen 24/7, I was trying to take advantage of easier days and follow a normal schedule as much as possible. That worked, until I needed to carry or lift anything heavier than a couple pounds—then I quickly became aware that nothing was normal.

Yet, there were plenty of things that hadn't changed one bit. I still enjoyed laughter with friends, the excitement of children (especially my grandkids), reading a good book, solving a complex issue, restoring a relationship, recruiting a gifted helper, and choosing the right fantasy football starter! Those are some of the pleasures that had always been part of my life, and continued to be.

During this time, I was listening to a message series, "In Search of Happy," by John Ortberg, a gifted communicator and pastor. In contrast to the happiness pursuit, he emphasized several ways to "make yourself miserable." One of them especially struck home for me: "Wait to be happy until your circumstances are just right."

Walking on the beach with my
portable oxygen concentrator

Even with my progressive illness I was still trying to control all the pieces of the puzzle so everything would fit "just right," and then I would be happy. I wrongly thought I could minimize the disruption of IPF in my life.

I became more accepting of my "new normal," while waiting for the unknown challenges yet to come.

3

CHECKING THE NUMBERS

One of my new "best friends" became a little medical device called a "Pulse Oximeter."

At any time I could pull this small, rectangular-sized instrument out of my pocket, slip it on one of my fingers and within seconds it gave me important information. With a tiny infrared light reading through the front of any fingernail, I was given the current oxygen content in my blood.

My readings when I was at rest were usually just a few points below anyone else—mid-to-high 90's. But where the Pulse Oximeter really helped was when I exerted myself, then I could quickly find out "how much, is too much." I then had several corrective options, ranging from breathing techniques to supplemental oxygen that I could use to get back to the right level.

This was very helpful because I could gain personal insight immediately about my oxygen levels. Plus, I could also use this objective data to reassure others that I was not over-extending myself.

I do remember wishing I could invent a similar device that could measure the condition of one's soul. A tool that could be slipped on the finger that gives us wise advice such as: "You are carrying way too much fear,"..."Your pride is in the danger zone,"..."Your greed is controlling you," etc.

To have a special instrument that could measure way beyond surface appearances and discern the inner rhythms of one's core being would be invaluable. Every person would know if they were being controlled by a condition that was slowly destroying them and could then make corrective decisions.

Unfortunately, such a soul-measuring tool does not exist, but I was beyond grateful that someone had invented a device to help me regulate my oxygen level.

O2D2

As Thanksgiving 2014 approached, I had another "best friend." I called him "O2D2"—which was short for Oxygen Delivery system when your lungs are in Decline. I seldom walked without "him" or some related version of portable oxygen. I needed him, and we became very close, but as I commented to Diane, "I get tired of how he is always hanging around!"

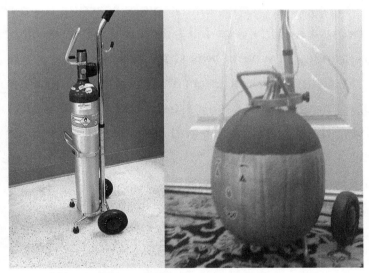

"Classic" O2D2 and a homemade "pumpkin spice" version which helped me win a Halloween contest at Rehab.

One of the minor benefits, of course, was that I no longer was getting judgmental stares about why I was parked in a handicap space. And I realized that in certain emergencies, with my back-up supply of oxygen, I would be just the right person to have around. I did find myself sitting and relaxing much more, because in doing so there was less need for an extra boost of oxygen. This became quite a balancing act because I knew I needed to keep my body active and strong.

As my lungs experienced more scarring from the fibrosis I would eventually need more supplemental oxygen, even when I was stationary.

With my dependence on O2D2, I found myself becoming more easily frustrated and impatient. Everything took longer, and I was regularly planning for a back-up supply. My "new friend" demanded my constant attention.

THERE GOES THE GARDEN!

The months passed slowly as my condition was periodically being monitored by my local pulmonologist. I was anxiously waiting to be called back to

The Cleveland Clinic to determine the timetable for this major medical procedure.

If there was one blow to my psyche, it was being told that I would have to give up one of my favorite pastimes, gardening, after receiving a lung transplant.

I enjoy nurturing seeds and young plants into beautiful flowers or delicious food and was very protective of my raspberry bushes, the hydrangeas, peach tree, and morning glories. It is fun to figure out what makes different plants thrive, to be able to change the conditions and then watch new growth take place.

I was informed that the reason I could not continue gardening in the future was because when working the soil, many microscopic spores, called *aspergillus* fungus fall from dead vegetation and are released into the air.

The normal person has an immunity to it and you breathe these spores in all the time without any impact. It is so microscopic that when it is released in the air, no face mask has a filter fine enough that would prevent someone who has had a lung transplant from breathing it in. There are cases where the condition was untreated and the transplant patient's health spiraled down rapidly. They were deceased in as few as three weeks.

Even with all the anti-rejection drugs prescribed for transplant patients, infection is a constant risk. So to give the new lungs the best chance for success, my future enjoyment of gardening would have to be experienced vicariously. Because of a compromised immune system, I would have to learn a healthy respect for the nature I love.

Giving up gardening was actually one of the easier changes I would have to make. I had to start thinking differently about my hobbies, my time, and my future. I really didn't have a choice in the matter. But if it meant I would have a greater chance of holding more grandchildren in the days ahead, I would gladly forego gardening!

BACK TO OHIO

Finally, some good news. The Cleveland Clinic had been monitoring my condition and wanted to see me again in the winter of 2014.

Another two days of intense scans and tests ensued. I learned that when they said, "A little pinch here," it meant whatever comes next was going to hurt for a short while but not be that painful. But when they warned, "Big pinch coming"—you would wish the test was already over.

I also figured out that when a schedule reads, "No food or drink for several hours beforehand," your visit with that doctor is probably not going to be "easy to digest."

My tests during this trip to Cleveland fell into two categories: (1) monitoring a specific aspect of my current condition, and (2) measuring any decline since the previous visit.

At the conclusion of the evaluations, I was told that since my last visit, my lungs had regressed into the "mild to moderate" range. I had shown a slow and gradual decline, rather than any sharp, "stair-stepping" drop that can be characteristic of many pulmonary fibrosis patients. They were pleased with my overall health and wanted me to keep being thorough in all aspects of self-care.

However, an increasing number of tests were done in preparation for what was yet to come...the major surgery of a lung transplant. These tests took detailed internal measurements as they checked for a list of things that, if present, would make an already delicate surgery even more difficult. The medical team places a really high value on keeping the surprises ahead to a minimum. In reality, they are also trying to determine which transplant candidates are going to have the fewest risks during and after surgery.

It was encouraging to learn that the transplant team continued to view me as an excellent candidate. "We will be having a major meeting here in a couple of weeks after all the data has been analyzed and will give you a full report."

I returned to Charlotte living in two realities: trying to stay as healthy as possible every day, while under the constant shadow of a life-changing surgery still to come.

HOW OTHERS SAW ME

By this time I was totally dependent on supplemental oxygen, which had a major impact on everyday life.

Most men aren't known to be great shoppers, myself included. It takes patience to browse for items that are not on my list to buy. If I am mentally prepared, I can shop with my wife through aisles of clothes, trinkets, and antiques knowing that we may not buy anything; we are "just looking." However, since I now needed to wear what is called a "nose cannula" and carry supplemental oxygen with me, it became even harder to shop, or just go out in public.

Initially I was quite self-conscious around others looking like I was hooked up to portable life support. That changed as I realized how quickly I became out of breath by just walking without my machine. Finding the right equipment gave me a lot more flexibility and freedom to go about a normal day. Then I needed to adjust my attitude and keep going out in public.

There really hadn't been any negative responses by strangers, but they usually fell into various categories. Here are several groupings:

Sympathetic Observers

Many realize that a person would not voluntarily choose to walk around on oxygen support, so there must be a medical problem involved. They would sneak a quick glance and then look away.

Curious and Quiet

This group of people kept looking back at me to

figure out what was going on with my whole situation. I sensed they were confused and trying to understand without prying or asking any questions.

Indirectly Inquisitive
Sometimes an individual would outright ask about my portable oxygen concentrator. Usually they knew someone who had used heavy tanks that needed refilling, so this new system was intriguing to them.

To the Point
After some initial introduction, this person would ask a direct question. They wanted to know more about my health issues that required this extra physical support.

Silent Supporters
These individuals would hold a door or defer in some way that indicated they saw that I was "handicapped"—and they kindly offered simple gestures of support. I didn't especially like the offers because I didn't feel limited. However, it was nice to more easily walk through a crowd of people and see a path magically open up in front of me.

A "REVERSE CELEBRITY"

Being out in public with a supply of oxygen attached to you definitely attracts some extra looks. More than once I felt like I was going to be asked for verification that I had a discharge slip from a hospital. For fun I tried to hold the door open for other people when entering or exiting a store. I found that very few could accept that gesture from someone who is connected to supplemental oxygen. They exhibited amazing gymnastic moves just so they could hold it open for me, even though I was naturally in position already. (My definition of fun was quite limited during those days.)

These responses made me much more empathetic to what famous men and women must face constantly when out in public. I was more in a "reverse celebrity" status (no autograph requests and no pictures snapped), but it was annoying enough to make me consider "just how badly do I want to go out?" At this stage of my decline I was choosing to stay home more often than not.

I have always preferred to be more a "behind the scenes" type of guy. I don't shun the public spotlight, but I don't need it, and seldom seek it.

To be wearing a device that so visibly made me different and drew attention bothered me. I would have preferred to have more control over my "first impression."

I think that strangers often saw me as a borderline medical emergency who was out and about getting some exercise. While I knew the real truth about my condition, others did not.

NOTES FROM KIDS

What brought smiles to my face and heart were the many cards, notes, and faith-filled prayers from children in our church family. Their handmade get-well wishes were incredibly special:

- "Hope you get well. My brother wants you back!"

- "I love you and am praying for you. Remember Proverbs 18:10, 'The name of the Lord is a strong tower; the righteous run to it and are safe.'"

- "Even though you are very sick, God is right there by your side and He is suffering it with you."

- "I heard about your condition and I am praying that you can get through this. If there is anything you need at home, I would be happy to help. (I am especially good at dog walking.)"

I was delighted and so appreciative for the prayers and expressions of love I received from every child!

4

THE WAITING GAME

The results from my winter appointment at The Cleveland Clinic were in, and if grades were given, I would have received an "A" for my overall health. While there was a slow and steady decline of my lungs, I definitely wasn't "next" for a transplant.

There would be future team meetings by the staff and I would eventually be given a number—my Lung Allocation Score (LAS). That score is determined by an equation using my breathing tests' results while factoring in other issues they had found that affect transplant readiness. It's kind of like golf, the higher the number the worse you are. If they determine my score is in the mid-50's or higher, I may be looking at the possibility of a transplant in a few months. A number in the 30's or lower will tag me for "more waiting,"—while they closely monitor my health and update the data.

I didn't mind being a bad golfer, but I wasn't quite ready for a high number on my LAS.

With a lung transplant, the need for donor lungs far outweighs the availability. Within the regions of the country you have to figuratively wait in line while your LAS continues to climb.

The size of your chest cavity is one of the top factors in finding a donor match. The more average your height and weight are the greater potential pool of candidates for a donor. The doctors will tell you there is an optimum window of opportunity that they are trying to match. They have a process of determining your decline and matching it with the best available lungs when you're at the worst, but haven't declined too far.

I would sometimes reply to people who asked how I was with, "I've declined overall since we last talked but the doctors say I'm not bad enough." Of course, such an answer is confusing to most individuals.

It takes emotional toughness to be able to feel

and see the weekly decline in your health, the greater need for oxygen, and the things that I was suddenly unable to do. To be honest, it takes a toll.

There are plenty of sobering statistics concerning the success rate of lung transplant surgeries. My doctors had all been "kindly direct" about the percentages and realities. The numbers are easier for me to talk about personally than to write out and actually look at.

I would have loved to have the cure without the risk, but that is not how life usually works.

MEETING REAL RECIPIENTS

Every few months it was back to Cleveland for more tests. My "score" was increasing—which meant that I was slowly getting worse and had moved up in priority for possibly being "listed" to receive a transplant.

My chart was filled with details and statistics from chest X-rays, to verify the size of the lungs and the chest cavity, pulmonary function tests, high resolution CT scans, bone mineral density scans, cardiac stress tests, and so much more.

During one visit I met several other pre-transplant candidates and heard a little of their stories. It made me realize that this is not a numbers game or just a simple score to be recorded and compared. Other men and women with hopes, dreams, and families would continue waiting when I was chosen. I didn't know all their names but I began to pray for them, wanting each one to receive a new set of lungs.

I was told repeatedly that after a successful transplant the focus turns to staying healthy and free from infections in order to avoid organ rejection. At the clinic I met a successful transplant recipient who, after two years, had chosen to be extremely cautious in all his exposures. While talking with him, I learned that since his transplant he never goes to a grocery store, attends a movie, doesn't shake hands, or even loan his pen. He admitted that he is following instructions to the "letter of the law," but it raised a lot of questions about my future choices. I couldn't imagine living in that much of a protective "bubble."

BREATHE DEEPLY

Go ahead. Take a deep breath and let all your air out slowly. Do it again and enjoy.

You probably take this simple luxury for granted, but actually, there are very few things you do that are more important than breathing.

During my months of waiting, I would have loved to have inhaled a deep breath again. I was told that this would be one of my greatest joys after the surgery.

Until then, I had to endure an "inner squeeze" if I tried to inhale deeply. My whole chest would tighten as my lungs fought back against the natural call to expand. My mind was thinking, "If I quickly try again the next one will be a full breath," however, the constriction from scarring was too much and the Idoiopathic Pulmonary Fibrosis (IPF) "python" wins again!

The competitor inside me doesn't like to lose in anything, yet the realist in me decided to fight back in other ways.

My doctor and hospital visits usually included several lung function tests that required me to breathe deeply and then exhale. To add to the torture a "clothespin" was placed on my nose so everything exhaled can be measured—since the only escape path is out the mouth. My lungs rebelliously kicked back with involuntary coughs, yet there was no reprieve.

"Let's try that again," are dreaded words, no matter how nicely spoken.

Before my next doctor visit, I was able to choose another motto. Instead of trying to "breathe deeply," I had discovered a new slogan while on a special "vacation."

Because of the kindness of our church family and after many years of full-time ministry, I was able to enjoy a refreshing sabbatical. Part of the time was spent in the beautiful state of Maine, which is especially stunning as the explosion of fall begins earlier than the calendar declares.

As we crossed the state line and pulled into the Welcome Center, we were greeted with these words: "Breathe easy, you're in Maine."

Now that was a motto I could focus on: "Breathe easy!"

TREASURED GIFTS

The holiday season of 2015 rolled around faster than I expected, yet I savored every moment.

I came to realize that the traditions and memory making around Thanksgiving and Christmas are enjoyed and felt more deeply when battling a serious illness. The gift of time spent with a longtime friend is treasured. An uninterrupted conversation filled with laughter, listening, and love is priceless.

There are many sick men, women, and children fighting very tough battles on a daily basis, and as challenging and limiting as my health crisis was, I often felt like I had a sprained ankle compared to the illnesses others were forced to confront.

But no matter what the diagnosis, if a person is supported with caring friends and family, there is an encouraging resolve and strength. We can't always generate enough positive energy by ourselves when coping with a serious illness.

Allow me to say this to those of you who are enjoying the priceless gift of good health. Take care of yourself! Understand the needs of your body, which include what you eat and your choices.

I am surprised how many people live in dread

of what illness they may face in the future, which is a negative way to exist. Exercise, eat wisely, and pursue healthy decisions in every area of your life. You will be stronger to face challenges and to be of help to others along the way.

While I am on this soapbox, allow me to remind you that the well-being of your soul is much more important than your physical body, so be sure your spiritual house is in order.

Since we live in a world where violence and tragedy will continue to bombard our newsfeeds and may even intersect with our own path, I pray we respond by increasing our love and care for others in need. Rather than withdraw and pull back in fear or fatigue, step forward and encourage those who you are prompted to assist. In doing so you fight against the same evil that has erupted in the most recent headlines.

AN UNEXPECTED CALL

"Mr. Cox I am calling to inform you that after reviewing your case the doctors have decided to list you for a lung transplant."

I was speechless. Had I heard correctly? I had prepared to hear those words sometime in the new year of 2016, but not three days before Christmas.

My case review had been delayed because of my continued strong test results, and many different care providers thought it was very likely that I was still "too healthy" to qualify for a lung transplant. To now hear that I was going to be "listed"...I could hardly believe my ears.

In an instant my mind and emotions had an internal collision that caused blank thoughts, a queasy stomach, 179 questions, excitement, confusion, and an overall inability to focus.

I pulled out a pen and began to jot down the information being given to me. There were some procedural next steps before the listing was official, but I was told, "Everything should be in order by early January."

I hung up the phone and cried.

It is very humbling to qualify for a lung transplant. There are scores of patients with this disease who for a myriad of different reasons cannot be approved for the procedure. There are many more who have died before they could get on the list. When your only known cure is a surgery that you are not eligible for, it's disheartening to say the least. However, even then it is too soon to give up. Your life can still have purpose and meaning as you fill it with lots of love.

To be honest, it is rather frightening to be approved for a lung transplant. My doctors had been very open and direct in preparing us for the realities of the surgery and life afterwards. One example was spoken to me as motivation to continue my current rehab routine so I could be as strong as possible in order to "recover from being hit by a car." (There was no mention of a seat belt or air bag. I think he meant in his word picture that I was walking when hit. I did find myself being more cautious when I crossed the street.)

Overall, I was excited about the timing of this unexpected news. Eighteen months earlier, we began fighting this disease with the goal of pursuing a lung transplant. There were many such recipients who were thriving with their new lungs, and in an unknown number of months I was planning to be one of them.

MY UPSIDE DOWN WORLD

On Thursday, January 7, 2016, it became official. My name was on the national lung transplant list. Until I received the next call, everything would remain the same. But in reality, my world had turned upside down. That is what happens when the "unexpected" strikes.

Just because I was on the "list" didn't mean there was a date for an actual transplant. There are many factors that have to fall into place—not the least being finding donor lungs that were a best match for my medical profile. To be "on call" for a major surgery is something you prepare for and then have to tuck into a corner of your mind. From any given minute of any day I could be six to eight hours from being flown to Cleveland and lying on a surgical table. To dwell on that reality messes with your day-to-day living, yet not to plan for it would be foolish.

My "waiting game" had just morphed to the advanced level. The donor process became much more personal. Yes, I was on the list, but I was also dependent on many details to come together before it was too late.

5

AREA CODE 216

I was in no rush to return home from work the afternoon of Friday, May 20, 2016.

It was a beautiful day—just the right amount of heat, humidity, and breeze allowed me to drive home with the windows down. I was sad that I was going to miss an upcoming retreat for elementary kids as they began to gather at the church buses.

The last few years I had been the speaker for this high-energy fun weekend with the students. Now I could barely creep to the car carrying my backpack. O2D2 was tagging along, flowing at 8 liters per minute (LPM), and I still had to stop once to catch my breath. Even my car crawled along as I drove through the pre-rush hour Charlotte traffic.

I didn't want to go home and face my four o'clock appointment. The oxygen supply company was delivering an additional concentrator to my house—that amazing device that takes in air and purifies it for those requiring medical oxygen due to low oxygen levels in their blood. That was me.

My increasing need demanded more than one concentrator could handle. I was hoping they would forget the appointment, yet knowing they had previously been annoyingly punctual in providing the life-giving oxygen my body was hungrily demanding, I doubted it.

The doorbell rang at 3:55. They quickly surveyed our existing set up and we determined the best placement for the new concentrator would be in the same downstairs dining room as the current one. The installer set it up, plugged it in, and then ran a short piece of tubing, splicing it with a Y connector to the existing tubing that was coming from concentrator number one. These "twin towers" dominated the room and provided life-giving sustenance in the form of air rather than food.

It was official. My organs craved oxygen more than the 10 LPM just one concentrator could provide. The disease had progressed to the point that more air sacs in my lungs were sticking together and gumming up...becoming useless.

The less my lungs were able to exchange the oxygen with carbon dioxide into the blood, the greater the need was for more supplemental oxygen being pumped into my body. Now it felt like I had a duet of concentrators, humming their constant droning noise. The tubing that snaked along the floor had a sinister-like appearance.

I remember sitting in the recliner and thinking, "This is a game changer."

Since I now needed 12 LPM of oxygen at rest and 15 when walking around, and since a portable oxygen tank, the kind that I used in my car, only pumped oxygen at 10 liters per minute—I was housebound.

SEARCHING FOR SOLUTIONS

Previously, when faced with a roadblock, I would mentally wrestle with it long and hard enough until a solution would be discovered. My proudest example was the creative way I ran tubing in my upstairs bathroom so that with just a little effort I could enter the shower, hook up to my nose cannula, all with minimal effects on my breathing.

Or another example: the two clips that I arranged on the stairs leading up to our master bedroom. They held the tubing in place which allowed me full access to the bedroom while staying connected to the concentrator below. "Can't" was not a word in my vocabulary.

Up to this point I had still been able to work and do my job a little more than 30 hours a week. But now I would no longer be able to drive to work safely, or even be *driven* to work.

My mind raced from one new problem to the next, but not the solutions. The only thing that was consistent was the noise of oxygen being forced into my nose faster than ever before.

I went to bed early, hoping a solution would come to life at the dawn of a new day. But Saturday brought more of the same as I sat in my recliner thinking of all the things I couldn't do.

A group of families from the church came over and helped my wife work in the yard. I wished I could help them but I had to stay inside—prefera-bly sitting down!

When the guests left, Diane asked what I would

like for dinner, and I quickly responded, "Strawberry pie."

It was early evening and our youngest son TJ, a recent college graduate, was bringing his usual energy and enthusiasm to the table as he finished grilling the chicken out on the deck.

A MIND-SCRAMBLING CALL

Suddenly, my ever-present cell phone was ringing. Area code 216 appeared on my screen. A number I knew well. This was Cleveland!

Time stood still. I answered the call with a tentative, "Hello."

"Mr. Cox, how are you feeling?" the voice of a young man greeted me. "We have a pair of lungs for you and I'm calling to coordinate flying you up here tonight for the transplant."

My mind immediately scrambled in a dozen directions. I tried listening to the instructions and found out:

- The plane would arrive around 10:00 PM.

- I could go ahead and eat anything I wanted.

- My wife could accompany me on the flight.

- We could bring two small suitcases.
- The Cleveland Clinic medical jet would be staffed with one nurse and flown by a pilot and copilot.

I explained my oxygen need was 12 LPM at rest. He told me, "Just take your time getting to the private executive area of the Charlotte airport and once on the plane we will have all the medical supplies necessary for the flight."

It was around 6:00 PM when I said goodbye and he told me to expect a call again with an update.

My wife and son heard my part of the conversation that we were headed to Cleveland that night and were eager and ready for anything. I was thrilled but have never been one to get overly excited too quickly. Plus I wanted to eat my dinner—and especially that strawberry pie!

Over the next few hours we followed our preplanned list of people to call and final details to arrange. We had held several family meetings in the months prior to this day, including our son Phil and his wife in California by video conference call, and had discussed every scenario we could think of or imagine.

THE U-TURN

Two weeks earlier we experienced a "live" practice. While traveling to TJ's graduation ceremony in Chattanooga, Tennessee, The Cleveland Clinic called to let us know that a donor lung match had been found and a plane was being sent. We were a couple of hours down the road, coming into Asheville, North Carolina.

We immediately made a U-turn and headed for home. Then, as we arrived back in Charlotte, in came a second call explaining that the donor lungs were not viable, so the flight was canceled. We spent the night in our own bed at home and arose early the next morning, making it to the graduation ceremony with thirty minutes to spare.

In the transplant world those are called "dry runs."

The Clinic had carefully communicated with us that we could be called, flown to Cleveland, prepped for surgery, yet at any point something could happen and the operation canceled.

I thought of my friend, David, who a couple years earlier, had experienced six dry runs in the span of a few months before the seventh was the actual transplant. His example reminded me not to assume anything but to prepare with every contingency in mind.

Our advance planning proved to be invaluable in making that Saturday evening very focused and calm.

A couple hours later, the coordinator called again. On the first ring I answered the phone. Everything was a go. He said, "The plane is being fueled up here in Cleveland and the crew is being readied for the flight. We need you and your wife to be at the business airport by 10:00 PM."

We arrived at 9:45.

The crew was concerned about getting me the short distance across the tarmac to the plane and up three steps without compromising my breathing. I promised I would walk slowly and that I wasn't worried about the steps.

It was an uneventful flight, and once we were in the air I was able to make a couple of follow-up phone calls with our son in California and his family. There wasn't a lot to be said, but I loved hearing their expressions of unconditional love.

THE CHECKLIST

I stared out the window into the starlight sky and went through my mental checklist:

- I had a disease that was only cured by a lung transplant.
- I had a condition where around 40% of patients die within two years of diagnosis.
- I was at 23 months and counting.
- Just the day before, my oxygen needs had changed and I would be limited to staying home.

Late night flight to Cleveland, May 21, 2016.

- I had passed all the stringent requirements of The Cleveland Clinic and was approved as an excellent candidate for the transplant.

My mind kept replaying a Bible verse from Isaiah 26:3: "You keep him in perfect peace whose mind is stayed on You, because he trusts in You."

I remember offering up prayers for the family who was dealing with a tremendous loss of a loved one at this time. It was an incredibly humbling moment. I remembered my friends that I had met in the two years since my diagnosis; both of them had passed away from this insidious disease.

In two hours our plane was circling back over Lake Erie with the bright lights of Cleveland below us. The yellow streetlights were giving off a warm glow. We were landing at a small business facility, Burke Airport, and I could see the police car waiting below to transport me to the hospital.

I was slightly disappointed when the nurse said, "We have plenty of time to get to the hospital, so the officer won't need to turn on the emergency lights and sirens!"

If I knew then what I know now, I would have lingered longer in the beautiful fountain courtyard of the main entrance to the hospital. But a wheel-chair was waiting for me and they had a plan. I was officially their patient.

The hallways were eerily empty and it was a short ride on the elevator to the eighth floor. I was "tagged" with my own wristband after confirming my name and birthdate.

At their request, I turned off my cell phone, handed it to my wife, and slipped into the hospital gown.

The tentative time for the surgery was set for Sunday morning, at 10:00 AM. It was also confirmed that this would be a double-lung transplant.

In the early morning hours there was a constant parade of different nurses and doctors doing their prep work. My arms quickly were dotted with IV's and PICC lines—which I had come to know as being connected to Peripherally Inserted Central Cathe-ter. Fluids in bags surrounded my bed and over my head. One of them dripped a light sedative that allowed me to drift in and out of sleep.

I could tell when daylight arrived as the room seemed brighter. The word came that all the trans-plant doctors were ready and the operating room was prepared.

A SPECIAL MOMENT

Our friends for over 35 years, Rob and Sara Quick, from Delaware, Ohio, joined my wife in the waiting room. Larry and Judy Masterson of Traverse City, Michigan, had driven through the early morning hours and arrived just before they rolled me back for surgery. They joined our oldest daughter, who had been able to change her weekend flight return trip. They all gathered together with my wife and prayed over me.

I don't remember the actual words that were spoken, but it was a very special moment as I literally felt the warmth of their love and prayers wrap around me.

I thought of all my children and grandchildren and my mom and dad, many of whom were already in the midst of planning trips to Cleveland.

I remembered our incredibly supportive church family back in Charlotte who would be attending a Sunday morning service. I smiled as I knew how God was going to hear the name Tim Cox constantly as word traveled to friends in various nations.

As they wheeled me away from the smiling, beautiful faces of my Diane and our friends, I remember thinking, "Let's get this done."

Friends and family gathered in the
waiting room during my surgery.

6

UNDER THE KNIFE

An anesthesiologist gave me some medication through an IV and I could feel myself becoming very drowsy. But my eyes widened as I was rolled into the center of the operating room with all the extreme bright lights glaring down on me.

I was intimidated and impressed at the same time. Nurses and doctors were talking to me constantly, telling me what they were hooking up or doing.

There was a pause and I could tell everyone was ready. The main surgeon, Dr. Usman Ahmad, then took my hand, looked me in the eye and said, "I am going to take good care of you."

Prior to my surgery, I had never met Dr. Ahmad,

but was very impressed with the fact that he had performed hundreds of such procedures. He is a native of Pakistan who completed an immunology and vascular biology research fellowship at the Yale School of Medicine's Vascular Biology and Transplantation program in Connecticut. His residency in general surgery was also at Yale, where he was named Educational Chief Resident in his last year of training. Dr. Ahmad completed his training in cardiothoracic surgery at Memorial Sloan Kettering Center in New York City.

Now, at this pivotal moment, I was comforted by his dark brown eyes, which latched onto mine and I felt an unspoken closeness—like it was just he and I.

Dr. Ahmad called for everyone to huddle around and I was asked to give my name and date of birth for the umpteenth time. No chance of operating on the wrong person!

Silently, I was praying for him and this team of doctors and nurses.

Then, speaking to his team, he reviewed what was just ahead. The last thing I remember hearing was the surgeon saying, "The patient is prepared; the lungs are prepared"...and he continued with some additional technical information.

A few more breaths and I could feel myself drifting away. I remember thanking God for my wife and also asking the Lord that if it be His will, I would live and hold my newest grandson who was due to be born in six more months.

TUBES, AND MORE TUBES

I had read enough about the procedure to know generally what was going on. A central venous catheter would be inserted into a vein to deliver fluids, nutrition solutions, antibiotics, or blood products directly into my bloodstream.

A tube would be placed in my mouth that goes down my throat and into my windpipe to help me breathe. And this same tube is attached to a ventilator that would mechanically expand my lungs.

Next, there would be a tube inserted through my nose and into my stomach to drain secretions, while another catheter was placed in my bladder to drain urine. There would be additional chest incisions where multiple drain tubes would be placed.

After all this, Dr. Ahmad would remove my old lungs and carefully replace them with the donor lungs.

My family was being given constant updates and was told that they were sewing in the left lung first since it was in the worst condition, and the right lung could carry me through that part of the surgery until it was replaced too.

The average time for a double lung transplant surgery is about 12 hours. Mine was completed in less than ten.

OH, THE PAIN

Coming out of surgery, my first thought was: *If I'm in heaven, the angels sure look a lot like my lovely wife!*

The second thought had to do with the overwhelming feeling of severe pain that pulsated through my body. But since I was still connected to a respirator that was helping my new lungs breathe, I couldn't talk.

In this painful medicated state, I recall Diane giving me the doctor's report she had received that the surgery had gone extremely well. The new lungs were working smoothly.

The respirator would remain in my mouth a

couple of days, which severely limited my communication, but it reminded my new lungs what their main duty was.

I drifted in and out of sleep. I remember trying to follow all the activity in the room as nurses were constantly checking or changing something.

Family and friends were being allowed to come to my bedside, but never more than two in my curtained cubicle at any one time. Our daughter Christina and our sons, TJ and Stephen, with his wife Liz, drove up from Charlotte and joined us the day after the surgery.

They took Diane out and found a one-bedroom apartment to rent as they planned ahead for my discharge. It was three blocks from the hospital and had clean rooms and wide hallways.

When our daughter Melissa was by my side, she had an uncanny ability to understand what I was trying to communicate that the other guests did not.

Whether it was a cold washcloth on my forehead or to swab out my dry mouth...with the smallest groans and a little eye contact, she immediately knew exactly what I needed.

The pain medications were being delivered

straight into my blood stream and I kept pushing a button for more relief. The nurses would usually give me a couple of minutes warning before they would carefully roll me onto my side to help prevent bedsores. This triggered new spasms every time, and yet they seemed to do it quite often!

However, the side effects of the powerful painkilling drugs are hallucinations. I later had to apologize to my son who I thought was adjusting my machines when it was really a male nurse with a similar build just doing his job! I was proud when I figured out on my own that the ICU room would not have insects crawling all over the walls...so I didn't comment when I would be the only one to see a "bug" quickly scamper across the ceiling and no one else seemed to notice or care. I finally mentioned it to my wife, and she came over late one night to sit with me until the imaginary bugs scurried away.

SURVEYING THE DAMAGE

I finally summoned the courage to inspect my wounds and was amazed at the clean lines of the incisions. Three 1-inch cuts halfway down each

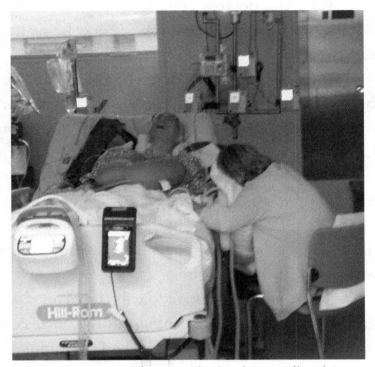

ICU recovery and fatigue. I had to hug a pillow lying on my stomach which helped when coughing. Diane faithfully sat at my side.

side of my chest had drainage tubes sticking out of them. Plus, there were two long lines that curved immediately under my chest about six inches long. The doctors had used those two openings to separate my ribs while removing my old lungs and sliding in the new ones.

After such a major invasion of my chest cavity I

remember the doctors coming in to inspect their work as some of the incisions were now being held together with glue.

I learned that my vocal chords had been damaged by the intubation, and what voice I had was very weak. A plastic surgeon came to my ICU room (along with many other spectators gathered around to watch him) and added more artificial tissue to my vocal chords.

There were constant X-rays, taken right in my hospital bed. But it required me to sit up, which was excruciatingly painful.

That first week, in the middle of the night, I was having a difficult time breathing, but the nurses' call button had slipped off my bed and was unreachable.

I prayed, "Lord, I need an X-ray so they can see what is going on inside."

At that very moment, I opened my eyes and the X-ray technician with all his equipment walked into my room. "Wow, that was quick," I thought.

It was like a heavenly moment where God assured me, "Don't worry. I've got this!"

BEEPS AND ALARMS

A few days after the surgery, I was able to sit up and stand, which seemed like major accomplishments. I began hearing about the possibility of being moved to a "step down" room at the hospital. It's given that name because it is a step down from intensive care, but not a general room.

However, Memorial Day was quickly approaching, and a vacancy never opened up in time for the paperwork to be completed that would allow for my transfer out of the ICU cubicle. The beeping of my machines were a constant annoyance, let alone when a next-curtain neighbor would have warning alarms also go off.

The step down unit sounded blissful. The rooms were more spacious and comfortable. Privacy, I had discovered, was an important part of the healing process.

At least the Memorial Day holiday brought in our good friends, Jeff and Nancy Alexander. The heavens parted and the waiting room "monitor" issued a divine decree that allowed an extra guest to my room and the four of us played cards—Kings on the Corners—from the small bedside table.

I recall feeling positive and upbeat as I was on

schedule for my targeted three or four week total stay in the hospital. I also remember feeling impatient, frustrated, and constantly hungry.

With the usual required stay of a few months in the local Cleveland area immediately after transplant figured in, I could still plan on being back home and in my own bed in Charlotte by fall.

The only comfort of home I had with me was my own pillow. Every nurse, it seemed, commented on that being a smart decision.

SOMETHING WASN'T RIGHT

Wednesday, June 1, dawned and I was excited. It was moving day. I tried to imagine my own "step down" room with a door that shut...and my own bathroom! Guests would be able to visit more easily, and I was promised a room with a view as a reward for my longer-than-usual stay over the holiday in ICU. Plus, I was approved for more normal food as my vocal chords were healing.

I was enjoying a small cup of peaches and sipping the syrup while they prepared to move me. My nurse was having difficulty removing the PICC line out of my right forearm and another came over to help.

I looked down, watching as they removed the needle, but something was not right.

A nurse pressed the Code Blue button and the on-duty medical team immediately rushed to my side.

I was barely conscious as I felt my bed being rolled out of the ICU cubicle. As they were transporting me, I heard a doctor in my left ear and my wife in my right ear—pleading for me to respond.

"Tim, can you hear me?"

"Please Tim, can you hear me?"

All I recall was feeling momentary confusion before I drifted into unconsciousness.

7

A LIFE-SAVING STROKE

I was told that the next four days were a whirlwind of activity and tests...all the while I lay there unconscious.

A CAT scan revealed that an air bubble had made its way into my bloodstream when the PICC line was being removed. I had suffered an air embolism stroke.

As Diane told me later, "Tim, I have never been so frightened. I thought I had lost you."

Nobody saw these complications on my horizon. They thought that once the surgery was over I would be on the road to recovery.

My right side was completely paralyzed except I

could move my lower leg and foot a little bit. While they were giving me a CAT scan, the doctor decided to check to see how my lungs were doing, which was more than providential.

Dr. Ahmad was miraculously in the unit when this emergency occurred. He took it upon himself to find Diane and confirm: "Tim had a stroke—and it most likely has saved his life."

He went on to explain, "The CT scan shows that there was a tear at the incision site, and if it had not been detected it would have caused both lungs to collapse and there would have been no way to revive him. Because of the stroke we will be able to correct a very serious problem."

The scan revealed a small separation occurring from the main connection to my trachea that would have slowly grown worse until, as Dr. Ahmad said, "He would have suffered a catastrophic event."

Since this was detected early, I was scheduled for a bronchoscopy the next day, and a stent was placed in the necessary spot for the connection to be fixed.

While the stroke had saved my life, I was still in critical condition and had not physically responded.

A BLINK AND A WIGGLE!

Our son Philip was already scheduled to fly in from his home in California. He was bringing our two grandkids, but now he had to tell them they couldn't come and see their Papa. He was by my bedside on Saturday morning, June 4, when he saw me blink and wiggle my toes.

I had awakened from the coma.

They quickly rolled me to an MRI unit for another brain scan. The report came back—no noticeable damage!

Diane rushed to be by my side, explaining everything that had happened. She started with the bad news. "Tim, you've suffered a stroke and your right side is paralyzed."

A sudden rush of emotions and confusion surged through my body. When she got to the part about how I had some movement in my right foot and lower leg I instinctively began to kick frantically. I was afraid if I stopped kicking I was going to permanently lose its use.

I also felt sick to my stomach as I instructed my brain to tell my right arm to move—but it just lay there by my side, useless.

The physician on duty had told Diane, "Patients who suffer this type of stroke usually recover and can function quite well, but every patient is different."

When she revealed the part of the story about my lungs and how the stroke had saved my life, I remember lying there, really still, trying to process it all. That lasted for about five minutes as I just couldn't accept that my right arm wouldn't do what my brain was telling it to. It was like my limb lay there laughing at me as I was trying to figure out where the instruction manual was that would tell my brain to lift my arm.

Finally, after several minutes of intensely focusing, my wife and I saw the tip of my right thumb move ever so slightly at my command. With her two good hands, she quickly texted our team of supporters to share this exciting news.

I fell back into bed exhausted.

Before I drifted off to sleep, I remember kicking my leg up and down as much as I could. Everything had just become much harder.

TOTAL DEPENDENCE

I knew things were really serious as another wave of friends and family traveled to see me. They came alongside Diane with the right emotional, spiritual, and physical support. Wonderful friends from Charlotte drove up when they heard about my stroke. The fact that their family name is "Saint" was appropriate as they helped Diane in countless ways.

I had my own ever-present nurse caring for me and watching all the machines. Phil also sat beside me and I benefitted from his expertise standing watch on his Navy ship. My doctors later told me they were impressed with his care and attention to detail.

I had to get stronger fast. It was excruciating, but I was ordered to sit up for as many hours as I could in the chair next to my bed. Yet I needed help with everything.

On top of it all, I was not allowed to eat, because when intubated the second time, damage was done to my throat and I now wasn't swallowing properly again. They hooked up a feeding tube through my nose which helped me receive nutrition, but it was adding to my aggravation. I finally was strong enough to move out of the ICU unit after a week. It was no longer a "step up" of celebration.

Movement returned to my leg, which responded more quickly than my arm. A physical therapist showed up to my room each day and performed his duties well. I learned to walk again as he held me up with a safety belt and I relied on a cane for support.

After a week I graduated from the safety belt but a nurse followed me with a wheelchair. Soon I was shuffling out of my room and walking down the hallway and back. Steve and TJ helped me with my daily walk, and our youngest daughter, Christina, brightened my room with her cheerful and encouraging spirit. No square inch of space was "safe" as she covered my room with cards and pictures.

By now I was attached to a more permanent feeding tube directly into my stomach. It was a daily parade of walking longer distances with my feeding tube by my side and a "spotter" in case I wobbled too much. A special day was walking to the break room at the end of the hall, catching my breath and looking out at the world, wondering if I would ever return to normal.

Once again, I had far more questions than answers. Little by little I was gaining strength, yet there was no mention of being discharged in the near future.

Finally, the plan was approved that I could be allowed to transfer to the Acute Rehab wing in another part of the hospital, referred to as M80—which stood for the eighth floor of building M—but not quite yet.

My lungs were improving, yet I couldn't get out of bed by myself because of the stroke. I needed assistance with everything. Getting dressed was a 25-minute ordeal. Brushing my teeth left-handed was messy but right-handed was impossible. I felt like a bird with a broken wing.

"Use it or lose it" was the new mantra that summed up my life as I tried to regain a range of motion on my right side. I did, however, have a clear breakthrough when I realized that my recovery was going to be at least 90 percent mental. The pain and limitations of the physical were directly impacted by what I was telling my mind.

I was receiving tons of support and encouragement from the doctors, nurses, and family members, plus the stack of cards and letters boosted my morale tremendously. But until I believed in myself and made the mental choices to override and push beyond the physical limitations I was going to be stuck in a state of limbo—an uncertain period of waiting for resolution.

PERSEVERANCE

During those days, when I was weak in strength and wounded in spirit, God brought back to my mind a sermon that I preached years before about the word "perseverance." My study of the term and its usage revealed that the best definition to capture the action part of perseverance was "to stay under while moving onward."

To truly persist and keep on keeping on means more than passively enduring some event. There were things to be done and actions to be taken!

I preached myself the same sermon for several days in a row. I was really motivated to be promoted to M80.

Since I needed to be escorted on any walks down the hallway I was limited to the availability of family members and nurses to accompany me. When no one else was available I remember making up exercises that I could do in bed.

Did you know that when you fold your hands together in a clasp, that's a learned behavior? I was practicing in bed one day spacing my fingers between each other and folding my hands in my lap when a doctor suddenly appeared at the door. She quickly mumbled an apology, looked away, and was walking out the door when I realized she thought she had interrupted my prayer time.

I called her back in and showed her my latest exercise. Together we shared a good laugh.

By this time, it had only been three weeks from the date of my lung transplant and my body was still adjusting from the surgery and the stroke. I was adapting to all the new medications and some days I would just feel plain lousy...and days were the best part. As the night staff would rotate in, I would begin to wonder about sleeping. Some nights, for no apparent reason, I could not fall asleep. If only tossing and turning could be considered an exercise!

THE CAVS AND THE INDIANS

That June I thought of myself as a good luck charm for the Cleveland Cavaliers and their world championship NBA run. The Cleveland Clinic is a major corporate sponsor of the Cavs, and their push through the playoffs was a basketball milestone, if not a miracle.

Also, that summer and the fall of 2016, because of my late night cheering, I felt I personally willed the Cleveland Indians to such a great record in baseball, almost winning the World Series. (Sorry Cleveland, the good luck charm of my presence apparently didn't work on your football team!)

It's ironic: the more you think about sleeping, the less you actually sleep. When I did nod off, invariably a machine alarm would accidentally start beeping, or I would wake up needing help to go to the bathroom, or a nurse would come in needing to prick my finger to check my blood sugar level. If the number was too high another nurse would soon follow to give me a shot of insulin. I soon learned that if you faked sleeping well enough and didn't respond to their quiet voice on first call, some of them would just back out of the room without testing your blood sugar or taking your vitals.

Praying for others would also help me relax and put things into perspective. Although I was one patient in one transplant center in one city of the world, new life was bursting all around me—even if death was also present. Every day I would hear the arrival of the hospital helicopter and imagine the life-saving organs being delivered or a patient being transported.

IPF is a rare disease, but there are many others just as serious and debilitating. The accounts I heard of patients being treated made my condition feel minor league in comparison. There was always someone far worse off than me. The stories of children especially were difficult to process, and praying for them often had the unintended consequence or benefit of relaxing me, and I would drift off to sleep.

My best time to catch a few uninterrupted z's were from 3:00 to 6:00 AM. After that, the portable X-ray machine and technician made his rounds with a daily scan of my lungs, which meant a cold, hard board stuck down between my back and the warm, soft bed. And I can't forget the feeding tube running 24/7, pumping nourishment directly into my stomach. If those bags ran out, a warning bell would sound. Or the feeding tube may plug up all of a sudden and start draining all over my bed. If this happened in the middle of the night, the sheets would have to be changed.

The nurses were amazing; they could perform this sheet-changing task with you still laying in the bed. But no matter how skilled, it sure could ruin a good night's sleep!

After my surgery, I felt the most comfortable when the hospital bed was inclined. But my body would slide down until I couldn't straighten my legs. Since I had limited use of my right arm and my stomach muscles were still not healed, I was constantly calling for help to scoot me up on the bed. This was one of the many frustrations of being so dependent on others.

"I'M SORRY"

Medication had to be administered through my IV since I had not yet passed the swallow test. Those that only came in pill form, the nurses would grind up, add water and try to get them into the IV without plugging up the tube.

There was a daily parade of visits by doctors, respiratory therapists, physical therapists, and appointments in other areas of the hospital that I had to be transported to—and every four hours I had another test for sugar levels.

I also caught on a little to the language of nurses. They have three different ways of saying, "I'm sorry." The first one is spoken after they responded to an inconvenience or delay, like not being able to act quickly when my machine was incessantly beeping.

The second is spoken with a tone of "there's nothing I can do about it, but I'm sorry." It was usually said twice a day when they administered the anti-blood clotting medicine with a shot directly in my stomach. With the subsequent bruising my stomach quickly resembled a well-used red, black, and blue pin cushion.

The third type of "I'm sorry" is spoken with feeling and empathy and usually a facial grimace as they knew they had hurt me through some accidental slip-up of their own doing. There weren't many of those, but you remembered them longer.

Looking back, every hospital patient is deeply indebted to an awesome team of servants who are definitely not paid enough for what they are asked to do.

One of the unexpected bonuses of being at The Cleveland Clinic was that I could sign up for a "musical therapist" to come to my room and present a personal mini-concert. The talented woman and I shared the same faith. It was awesome.

The second time she came and blessed me with a performance, there were several doctors trying to enter my room, and they weren't too happy when I told them, "You'll have to wait. She was here first."

Those visits proved to be powerful times of praise and worship I will never, ever forget.

8

LAUGHTER, SWEAT, AND TEARS

There was one phrase I dreaded to hear: "Tim, it's time for another bronch."

Bronch was short for bronchoscopy, and they were giving me one every couple weeks. A doctor specializing in this procedure goes down my throat into my lungs with a tube that has a camera, lights, and instruments. While in there they can perform many different procedures and tests on the lungs.

In my case, different sized stents were needed in five locations in the bronchi airways to keep them open.

The procedure can detect tumors, signs of infection, excess mucus in the airways, bleeding, or blockages in the lungs. It can also allow the doctor to take samples of mucus or tissue for other laboratory tests.

For me, immediately following a normal bronchoscopy, my breathing was smooth. But soon it would become rougher, and loud enough to be heard.

I learned that I was one of the 20 percent of transplant patients who develop this condition, called "stenosis of the lungs."

The word "stenosis" simply means *narrowing*. So in my case, I had a stenosis of the pulmonary airways. Every person is different in healing and in responding to the stents.

WAITING FOR REHAB

My goal for the month of June was to get stronger and be promoted to M80 rehab—the final frontier for my ultimate objective of being discharged from The Cleveland Clinic completely.

Even though my family and I were all anxious for our ordeal to be over, we had no idea how long we would need to be in Cleveland. There were still medical hoops to jump through before my doctors were confident enough to release me.

The highlight of each day was when Diane would bring the mail and we would read it together. I finally was regaining my strength enough to have my phone and iPad back so I could, in small doses, keep in touch with the outside world.

The July 4 holiday came and went without my promotion to M80, but I did get my taste of real food—a couple bites of a popsicle, which my stomach wasn't ready to handle.

Holiday hours in a hospital are like treading water; the staff is still working, but unless you have a life-threatening need, it feels like you're just maintaining. The Clinic has a rooftop patio that offers a panoramic view of the downtown and Lake Erie. I loved going up there, but as intoxicating as the fresh air was, it was also exhausting. I had lost a lot of weight and no wheelchair is comfortable even with extra padding.

I tried to play board games as part of my rehab for my right hand movement. More than once it was discouraging to see the tremors in my right hand as I tried to move my pieces or pick a card. Fortunately, family and friends would joke about it and straighten out my trail of messes.

PANIC AT M80

A promotion or a transfer in any hospital is a process of obtaining the right signatures on the paperwork and that usually takes several days. So I learned to control my enthusiasm and excitement when I heard that moving to the rehab facility would soon be a reality.

I had improved enough where I could more intensely focus on the use of my right arm and leg.

Finally, I was moved to M80 on Thursday, June 23.

Friday was exhausting but exhilarating as I had two one-hour sessions with different therapists focused on retraining my body to find new mental pathways for my muscles on the right side to respond the way I wanted. Then I would return to my room, be hooked up to my feeding tube, and fall into bed.

That same night I was having serious difficulty breathing. And when the therapist arrived, I forced myself to the morning session but my energy was depleted and each breath was becoming harder by the minute.

I was wheelchaired back to my room and slept

for a couple of hours. But before my next appointment, it took me five minutes to recover from walking just five feet from my bed to the wheelchair.

Whatever was going on inside me just didn't feel right.

They canceled my second rehab appointment that day and suggested more rest. "We'll see how you feel on Sunday," I was told.

Sunday was worse. A doctor came in, listened to my lungs, and reported, "They sound clear as a bell."

But at that point, every breath I took was rough and labored. I was laying in bed wondering, "What next?"

Diane panicked when she visibly saw my heart pumping erratically from a few feet away. She called The Clinic's internal 911 phone and that alerted an emergency team to evaluate the situation.

Suddenly, my room became alive with doctors and nurses. New tests were immediately ordered, and by Sunday night I was moved back to a corridor in the area I had come from three days earlier so they could hook me up to the machines that allowed for closer monitoring.

Breathing treatments helped a little, but there was a blockage occurring somewhere. It was determined that I needed another bronchoscopy to check out what was going on in the airways of my lungs.

Then I was told, "Mr. Cox, the first available time is on Wednesday."

Between ragged breaths, I shook my head "No," and let them know that I honestly didn't think I could make it until Wednesday.

The doctor asked, "Are you sure?"

I only had the strength to nod, "Yes."

Thankfully, the physician was convinced and they found a time slot on Tuesday.

I have no idea what my "Bronch doctor" had planned for his Tuesday evening, but that all changed when he took a look inside my airways. They were aggressively healing themselves—but not in a good way. They had almost closed off completely.

It took him and another bronch specialist two and a half hours to reopen my airways and strategically place the life-saving stents.

Later, he told me, "I don't know how you were even breathing."

They kept me totally monitored for the next several days before allowing me to move back to M80.

THE MENTAL STRUGGLE

The next two weeks were spent in laughter, sweat and tears...and not always in that order. There were tears of frustration as I flunked another swallow test—which meant a close relationship with the feeding tube and the ever-present bag of liquid food hanging over my head was going to continue.

My laughter was at my own expense watching my body try to do the simplest of tasks, like slipping wooden rings over pegs. It was therapeutic child's play, yet frustratingly hard. When I became too discouraged, I would look around and notice that I was one of the advanced students in the session.

I had much to be thankful for compared to many other patients. But I thought, "How crazy that I have to relearn the common movement of swinging my arms while I walked." It just doesn't naturally happen. It is a series of commands that we take for granted until the mental pathway is blocked.

There are mirrors everywhere in rehab units so you can watch your good side do what you want, while you tell your brain to reroute the commands and instruct the weak side, "Do that."

I was constantly reminded that the mental battle

was greater than the physical, by far. Patients all around me were struggling with the realization of the hard work it was going to take to regain lost movement—and often not to the same level as before their tragedy.

Many refuse to engage; for them the change had been too drastic, too quick, and the road back was too far to imagine. The physical therapists were actually, in varying degrees, motivational psychologists. Sadly, however, they were losing the battle for some patients' minds and will.

In one session, a group of therapists asked me to play a game of beanbag toss at a target just a few feet away. It was obvious that they wanted me to help set an example for the other three men in their group to strive for.

First round targets were set an equal distance away for all of us. I went last, and compared to my opponents, I looked like an Olympic athlete.

In the second round, only my target was moved back farther than the others. The results were similar as I adjusted to the new length and focused on improving my own strength.

I was hoping it was over, but our young therapists proudly announced, "We have time for the third and final round."

They were not noticing the opposite effect this game was having on the motivation of the group. So I took things into my own hands and both literally and figuratively threw the game. I "somehow" lost that round and got out of there as soon as possible.

LIFE AT #502

Finally, D-Day came—as in Discharge!

On Friday, July 29, 2016, I was given the okay to join my wife at our Cleveland apartment. After 69 days of x-rays, tests, shots, breathing treatments and too much HGTV...I was going to once again be part of the outside world.

Diane and other assistants helped me to our car that was parked in the same courtyard where I had been dropped off in the middle of the night by a police cruiser ten weeks earlier. The sound of the fountain was soothing; a welcome noise compared to the beeping of machines and monitors.

At the apartment complex, we took the elevator to the fifth floor. Diane unlocked the door to #502, and proudly showed me our temporary one-bedroom suite.

When I walked through the door, the "quiet" was so soothing that I broke down and cried. I was exhausted, but relaxed and extremely happy.

This new environment watered the seed of hope that I was going to fully heal and return to Charlotte—perhaps in the not-too-distant future.

For the next few weeks, life at #502 could be characterized as two steps forward, three steps back.

I avoided mirrors because my 120 pounds was not a look I wanted to see. I was approved to have soft foods and broths, and was more than thrilled when I finally passed my swallow test.

Every week I returned to The Cleveland Clinic for appointments or tests—and the bronchscopies were now being stretched beyond every three weeks.

During a bronch in late August, my doctor determined that healing was happening so well at one spot in the airways that he could remove a particular stent.

I wish it had worked out, but my airway was not ready to support itself and I ended up back in the hospital for the weekend until they replaced the stent and my breathing returned to normal.

The highlights of the first few months were eating every meal, haircuts, peaches, visits from family and friends, my wife's chicken and dumplings. I also enjoyed drafting my fantasy football team with my senior pastor who flew in with his wife for a quick visit, and being an encouragement to one of my neighbors in the apartment building who was battling with IPF while waiting for a donor match.

The "low lights" included exhaustion from simple things like trying to tie my shoes or trim my own fingernails. Then there was the stabbing pain in my side as the scar tissue healed. I also experienced frequent sleepless nights and random days where I felt totally sick for no reason. And rehab was a necessary evil!

What pulled me through the first few months was the daily encouragement and love from my incredible wife, family, and friends, combined with all the prayer support from around the world.

I must admit, however, that our positive attitude was stretched to the limit and dealt a triple blow in late October.

That's when Diane and I learned from our doctor that we were going to have to remain in Cleveland through the winter. I needed bronchoscopies too frequently to make the drive from Charlotte. On top of that, I needed more isolation instead of getting back to a public life at home. They explained that the flu and cold season must be taken seriously if you are a transplant patient...especially lungs. A sneeze from a few feet away could be the start of a bad cold, which could turn into pneumonia and compromise the new lungs. I was clearly not yet out of the woods.

FACING THE COLD

In early November I went in for another routine bronchoscopy. Once more, they believed I was improving and a stent was removed.

It was a repeat of what had occurred in August. The next morning I was gasping to find my next breath. When breathing is difficult you don't want to exhale; you just keep trying to only inhale until your need for oxygen is satisfied. But that is not physically possible.

I was in the next room, laboring for my breath, when my training kicked in. I made it back to the side of my bed where I could more easily sit up, take deep breaths, and do a breathing treatment.

Diane called for an ambulance. I didn't see any other way to get to the hospital as all exertion would leave me gasping for breath. It was embarrassing to be so close to The Clinic yet in need of an ambulance, but there seemed to be no other choice.

The X-rays revealed that my right lung was swollen and enlarged. Air was slowly getting in, but could not get back out to exchange it and exhale. They placed me on a CPAP machine (which stands for Continuous Positive Airway Pressure). And I had a full face mask.

When the stent was replaced, I was back to semi-normal.

The doctor could see we were not pleased with the thought of winter in Cleveland. It wasn't that I feared the snow and cold of a normal Midwestern winter, this was South compared to where my childhood home was in northern Michigan. I was bothered at the thought of being so far removed from friends and family and the extended support system we had at home.

So I was approved for a visit to Charlotte on my birthday weekend in November. It was the boost we both needed. I could be a full-time father, papa, and friend from the comfort of our home, if even for just a few days. I got to see our oldest daughter, Melissa, try on her wedding dress she had found for her Spring 2017 nuptials.

Even more of a highlight that weekend happened a couple days later when our son Steve and his wife Liz gave birth to our newest grandson, Carter Timothy Cox, born one day after my 59th birthday. It was very emotional moment when I held him for

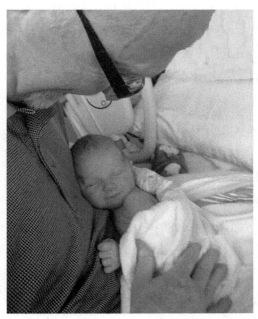

The answer to my pre-surgery prayer, Carter Timothy Cox, born November 21, 2016.

the first time...the answer to my pre-surgery prayer.

When it was time to board the plane for our return trip to Cleveland, it was with a renewed sense of purpose and challenge for the winter ahead.

A SPRINGTIME DREAM

Permission to eat anything and everything I wanted made the Thanksgiving and Christmas season more than special.

We attended a very touching Donor Memorial Service at a Cleveland area church where testimonies were shared in honor of the donors who passed away so we might have life. What a final act of love they had made.

Thankfully, the winter of 2017 was a mild one. I had regained most of my weight to a pre-transplant level, but it was surprising how cold everything still seemed to me. The partial paralysis of my right side would be something I would have to live with, but at least my bronchoscopies had stretched out to every five or six weeks.

The troubles of the fall and winter faded like distant memories as our daughter's wedding date approached. A week before her late-April marriage, we were once again making our way down the I-77 corridor to Charlotte —this time in our SUV, stuffed with items we no longer needed in Cleveland. We were not totally released, yet we knew the time was getting close.

Just two days before the wedding, Diane's phone rang from an unknown number in the 216 area code. What could Cleveland want?

It was Dr. Ahmad, who had performed my transplant surgery. He was calling to congratulate our family on the upcoming marriage and to let us know that he had tried to shoe-horn a flight into his busy schedule and surprise us by showing up at the wedding. It didn't work out, but we enjoyed the flowers and chocolates he had arranged to be delivered to our doorstep.

Even now, as I write about this, I am moved by such acts of thoughtfulness from this extremely busy man.

A SPECIAL CONNECTION

The wedding weekend was magical for me. Our daughter looked stunning, and the gathering of friends and family was both invigorating and exhausting.

One of the best decisions we made in our frantic fall in Cleveland was to reserve a beautiful house within a few miles of the wedding venue. It was large enough for all of our five kids and their mates and children to stay in comfortably.

After the rehearsal dinner and the grandkids were in bed, I hung onto our special family time late into the night. Finally, I couldn't stay awake any longer, yet didn't want that moment to end. Our bedroom adjoined the family room, and our children offered to take their party downstairs, but I would have none of it. I drifted off to sleep with the laughter of my family echoing through my mind.

In the thoughtful planning of Melissa and her husband-to-be, Zack, they had arranged for a candle to burn on stage during the ceremony in memory of my donor, and in honor and thankfulness of the donor family.

At the wedding reception I was asked to propose a toast to the newlyweds. I told Zack what a great listener Melissa was...and that she wouldn't always need words in order to understand him. I gave this illustration:

"It is normal for lung transplant patients to be intubated for a couple days after the surgery. With a breathing tube stuck down your throat, talking is not an option. And when you add the painkillers and their effect on my alertness, well, communication is difficult at best, if not impossible. That is when we discovered Melissa's hidden talent!"

Then I told the story of how Melissa had such an amazing way of understanding my combination of mumblings, moans, and motions, and with just a couple of questions was able to determine what I was trying to communicate. I continued:

"It still brings a smile to my mind as I think about that special connection.

That is what I hope and pray for the two of you...a super, special connection to last a lifetime, whether words are used or not. No matter what the future brings, may your deep and abiding love be communicated to each other and to this world...to everyone you meet!

As you share your love, may it grow and unleash a powerful cycle of loving deeds, emotions, thoughts, feelings...and sometimes even words! We all raise our glasses to toast to and pray for a future filled with love.

To Zack and Melissa!"

A proud dad moment...walking Melissa down the aisle on her wedding day.

THE STORY WENT VIRAL

That spring, The Cleveland Clinic asked their media department to film a short story documenting my journey and that I was alive to enjoy our daughter's wedding. It was part of their promotion of the annual National Donate Life Month, held every April.

A Cleveland television station picked up the story and came to our apartment to get some additional footage and interview Diane and me. Network affiliates and stations from across the country played different parts of the video for their viewing audience.

While I was still in Charlotte after the wedding, a local station sent over a reporter to tape their own interview with me—which I gladly agreed to since it promoted awareness of this rare disease.

After another taste of "real life" in the Carolinas, it was back to Ohio...hopefully only long enough to hear our doctor release us from having to live in Cleveland.

9

THE REARVIEW MIRROR

With the transplant almost a year behind me, yet still not released to resume life in Charlotte, I began to reflect on the ordeal I had endured.

It's human nature to categorize everything into either a "good" or "bad" list. We hear of an accident or a diagnosis of poor health and immediately put that event on our "bad news" list. If you are like me, however, you try to figure out a way to move this reality from the negative side to the positive.

When this doesn't happen, our mind wants to fall back to the age-old question: "How could God allow this terrible thing to occur?"

Although no one has ever audibly addressed that

question to me, I have seen it several times in the eyes of people who are trying to make sense out of my diagnosis. There is an awkward pause, a looking away, an offer of continued prayer, and a quiet moving on. The mental wrestling is obvious; their frustration is barely suppressed.

At such moments I began to wonder why I hadn't asked God, "Why?" I was far from a spiritual giant and my faith was often dangerously low. However, for some reason, I wasn't demanding answers—I didn't feel that God owed me an explanation about my condition.

I rested in the knowledge that He had everything under control.

ADVICE FROM EXPERIENCE

Since I had survived the transplant, I was often asked, "What advice can you offer to those who have been diagnosed with IPF so they will be better prepared for what is coming?"

After looking back in the rearview mirror, here are six specific recommendations that could be applied to almost every tragedy:

1. It's Always Too Soon To Quit

As I lay in a post-surgery hospital bed, there were many times I was tempted to justify the reasons I was having a "poor me" attitude. Then I would hear a story of a next-door patient who was still waiting for a lung to be found.

I was buoyed by the stories of people in difficult situations, and how they had persevered and overcome.

Instead of dwelling on the dark side of your circumstance, discover what inspires you, and focus your thoughts there. I pray what you are reading is enlightening and provides help.

The reason I didn't wave a white flag of surrender and give in is because I believe Almighty God is the God of all hope—and He can do anything at any time.

2. Make the Best Decisions with the Information You Have

There will be risks with every decision you make, but don't jeopardize your overall health while waiting for more answers before deciding on a treatment plan. Absolute certainty is rare and could be deceptive.

When Diane and I were weighing the options for where my transplant would be performed, a primary concern was finances. Although our first choice was a noted hospital in our state, it wasn't in the network fully covered by our insurance—making that option far more expensive. Thankfully we made the right choice.

3. Even in Your Weakness, Bless Your Caregivers

Of all the nurses who have taken care of me, a very high percentage have done an amazing job. They have been courteous, kind, and unbelievable servants. The exceptions have been few.

However, when you are on edge, even the slightest problem becomes magnified.

One night, about 2:00 AM, I needed help going to the bathroom. My stroke still limited me in getting out of bed, so I was required to press the call button for a nurse. There were different switches that controlled the lighting in the room, and almost all of the nurses would use a sidelight to give enough illumination to help me. But the nurse that came in this time chose to turn on the power for the surgical light directly above my bed and the room immediately went from dark to "interrogation lights."

As I shielded my eyes and turned away, I groaned in frustration "Aargh!" She snapped at me "What? I have to be able to see!"

Thankfully I was alert enough to think before responding and realized I needed her help to meet my need. I also had no clue what was going on in her life before she entered my room. So I said, "It's just so bright."

She responded, "Well, I need to be able to see." I chose not to say anything more as she helped me into the bathroom.

4. Make Your Peace with God

I realize that those who experience medical traumas come from a wide variety of religious traditions. My Christian faith has given me the assurance that even death is a victory for the man or woman who has made peace with the heavenly Father.

I recommend memorizing and praying the Lord's Prayer out loud. It is found in Matthew 6:

> *Our Father in heaven,*
> *Hallowed be Your name.*
> *Your kingdom come.*
> *Your will be done*

On earth as it is in heaven.
Give us this day our daily bread.
And forgive us our debts,
As we forgive our debtors.
And do not lead us into temptation,
But deliver us from the evil one.
For Yours is the kingdom and the power and
    the glory forever.
Amen.

This communicates our willingness to have God's will fulfilled through life or death. The perfect earth He created is not the world we live in today.

Personal, national, and global tragedies continue to take place on a daily basis and God will eventually make all things right. But until then, we must live with faith and trust.

5. Choose to Inspire Others

It is important and life changing to find someone to serve. All around you are single parents, special needs children and adults, military families who have a parent deployed, not to mention the lonely men and women struggling at a care facility near you.

You have the opportunity to bring community

to them, so introduce yourself and build a relationship. Serving others brings healing and strength. Remember, we are all in this together.

From the time I was diagnosed with IPF, Diane and I made a commitment to turn the spotlight from ourselves, and onto those who were either facing a crisis—or had a loved one who was.

I'm sure that my years of ministry had a huge impact on that decision, but I hope I would have responded the same, regardless of my background or training.

While I was in ICU, what kept me going was knowing that what I was able to share with my "curtain neighbors" might uplift their spirits and instill hope.

At the same time, Diane was in the lobby with distraught family members of someone undergoing surgery—holding their hands, wiping away tears, and offering prayers of support. To us, this was as natural as breathing (which had actually become *un*-natural for me).

This lifestyle continued at our Chester Street apartment building, where some of the renters were traveling a similar medical path. As I found out, ministry doesn't cease when you are in a "time out" situation. I tried to never be "off the grid."

The best part was that what we did for others, was reciprocated many times over.

One of the most memorable moments while I was in the M80 Rehab Unit was opening a small package that was sent to me from Charlotte.

Inside was a signed baseball and a note. It was from a Little Leaguer who attended the church where I was a pastor. He had hit a game-winning home run in the championship playoff, and told his mom, "Send it to Pastor Tim."

When I received it I cried tears of thanksgiving because someone back home was remembering me and knew this special gift would boost my spirit. I will never forget the thoughtfulness of that boy sending me such a treasured momento. I still have the baseball prominently displayed in my study.

6. Find a Trusted Friend to Help with the Paperwork.

Diane and I agree that one thing we would do differently is to find a person on our team who would have been willing to keep track of the monthly bills from the hospital, insurance company communications, and correspondence.

A small plastic wristband was the first thing

attached to my body before the surgery and never came off while I was a patient at the hospital. It was scanned before every pill taken, every breathing treatment, every test, and every doctor appointment in keeping track and totaling my bill.

Diane's days were filled to overflowing with my care, and I wasn't much help because of my condition. By the time we were able to respond to the charges, we were so far behind that we felt helpless and hopeless.

It will save you many frustrating, time-consuming hours if you can find a trusted friend or loved one who is willing to make phone calls on your behalf and follow up on mistakes, which do happen.

You may not have as long or as complicated a recovery as mine, but such a decision will free you and your caregiver to focus on the task of becoming stronger.

ROCK-SOLID

Many years ago, when I was in seminary, our professor of evangelism was a godly man named Oscar Thompson. After about five classes into the semester, it was discovered that he had an aggressive type of cancer, and an adjunct professor came in to finish teaching the semester.

At the final class, Dr. Thompson returned to the classroom. You could tell the curtain of his life was closing as they propped him up in a chair while he spoke to us.

I will never forget his words: "I've been to the bottom and want you to know that God's Son is rock-solid. He is the foundation you can build your life on."

Those words came back to me many times as I was laid low for so long. The storms of life are profoundly affected by what we believe. The details of what is currently causing you frustration, pain, and worry are different than mine but the antidote is exactly the same. In facing life's challenges, patiently persevere by doing what is right, based on God's Word.

Faith is stronger than fear, and is the daily fuel that powers you to victory.

HEADED SOUTH

Wednesday, May 31, 2017, was a red-letter day on

our calendar. That's when my doctor, Marie Budev, spoke the words I had been longing to hear: "Mr. Cox, every target of your recovery has been reached. You are free to go home."

A hugging party ensued as we tried to thank her for the hours of attentive care and love she had provided ...and still provides.

After exactly one year and ten days, we were so ready to go home that we came to the appointment with our car already packed.

Early the next morning, June 1, we were headed south again. With great anticipation, we were only looking forward. In reality, our SUV was stuffed to the ceiling so that looking in the rearview mirror would have been useless. Besides, we had seen enough of Cleveland for a while.

We would once again be full-time residents of Charlotte, and yet the lessons we had learned had changed us forever.

Although impressed with the people and city of Cleveland, in many ways we had seen enough for a while.

10

THE FINISH LINE

In any life tragedy, it is vital to surround yourself with two types of individuals: (1) right thinkers and (2) positive people. You will need both as you absorb the facts of your setback.

Right thinking about the situation without a positive upbeat attitude feels cold and hard-hearted. On the other hand, an always cheery and optimistic outlook wore on me quickly and didn't feel realistic considering the serious life and death reality I was facing.

You will be surprised by the responses of people. I'm still amazed that some I thought I was very close to have, to this day, never mentioned anything about my disease, my treatment, my lung transplant, or my absence, other than "Glad to have you back in Charlotte."

Thankfully, those moments are rare.

When you first begin talking about an illness or condition, be prepared to hear about at least one recommended treatment or "home remedy" per week. So get ready as to how you will respond. If you want to pursue one of them because it sounds plausible, then pass it on to your core team of right thinkers. Ask them to research and advise you about its legitimacy.

Your life will be consumed with doctor appointments and new medical terms. It's as if you are learning a foreign language. So right thinking about your new physical realities is going to be tougher than you thought. Embrace, accept, even hate it. But refuse to allow the truth to immobilize you.

Surround yourself with your team and welcome their offers of help. Even if to date you have been tragedy free, there are things you can do and *should* do. If you are married, spend as much time as you can, expressing your love and building the strongest relationship possible with your spouse. In your community, develop quality friendships and nurture them; your life will be enriched whether you face a crisis or not. Then, if you should be surprised by tragedy, you will have a built-in support system and a team.

AVOID ANALYSIS PARALYSIS

Within days of my initial diagnosis, I can recall being in my backyard, crying out loud, "I want my life back."

Thankfully, God didn't listen to my plea as I have changed for the better in so many ways through this unexpected journey.

I learned to avoid paralysis by analysis. Some decisions will need to be made without the advantage of every detail or fact. Talk it through with your team and take your best option. Seek counsel from as many people as you have time for and take the matter before the heavenly Father. Just realize that at some point you are going to have to act in faith with the facts at hand.

You are your own best advocate and know better than anyone else that your health is affected by the decisions you make. Pray for your miracle, then find out what actions you need to take—and do them.

Never stop living, loving, and laughing. I felt the

most healthy when I was laughing until I cried with family and friends.

Usually there is an exhaustion that sets in with your illness, so find your "best energy" times and fill them with the highest priority items on your "to do" list. Pace yourself for the long-haul and review your plans from time to time. Then adjust accordingly.

Within six months of my diagnosis, two new drugs were approved in the treatment of IPF. More proof of their effectiveness was found in Europe and Canada than in studies in the United States. They were not offered as a cure, but had shown results in some patients at slowing the scarring down from its fast pace through the lungs. I weighed all the factors and finally decided "yes" when a specialty pharmacy offered to underwrite almost all of the monthly cost. In my case, side effects were signifi-cant, and yet over time I adapted. I took the drug for about 16 months and only went off it at the advice of my doctors when I was approved to be on the transplant list for new lungs.

FIND A DAVID

One of my best decisions was to follow up on an introduction to a person who lived a few miles away who had a double lung transplant two and a half years earlier. I mentioned him in an earlier chapter, but David became my lung mentor, and he graciously made himself available at anytime for my questions.

He reminded me that his story was not my story—since mine was in the process of being written. Time and time again he would be the antidote for some real pain or irrational fear that I was feeling. There's nothing like having a David in your life—or being a David if you are at that stage of your journey.

THE FAITH FACTOR

My long life of faith in God was shaken to its core, but by His grace I withstood this test.

Pre-transplant, the nights were really confusing as whispers of doubt creep into your mind. Verses of Scripture I had memorized long ago were the only weapons that would work in stopping the taunts to my faith. Yet there was that distressing detail that someone would have to die at the right time, with the right size lungs, and the right blood type before the exchange of life could take place.

NEVER FORGET YOUR DONOR

When I lift my voice to sing, it is with the help of lungs that aren't even mine. Through the generous donation of an anonymous family and by the sustaining grace of God that has been poured into my life, the doctors exchanged my diseased lungs with healthy ones.

I still find it difficult to adequately honor the donor family whose loved one died that I might live. No words can be written or spoken to cover their grief, yet because of their loss, I am able to breathe again.

The identity of donors and recipients is seldom revealed, although anonymous letters can always be exchanged through a third party.

I have written a letter of gratitude to my donor family, whoever they are, to tell them about the grandchildren I've been able to hold and the candle that burned brightly in honor of their loved one's memory at my daughter's wedding...all blessings I have since enjoyed because of the sacrifice.

I cannot express enough "thank-you's."

THE ULTIMATE EXCHANGE

I will never be able to erase from my mind that I have continued my life because of the death of another human being and their willingness to donate their healthy lungs to a complete stranger. The parallel is not lost on me with the truth of Jesus Christ who died over 2,000 years ago to meet my need for a Savior and the personal healing that only His forgiveness provides. That restoration transformed my heart of stone to a heart of flesh, and the exchange reminds me of His promise to make all things right—back to the way He originally designed them to be.

My Ultimate Mentor said, "I am leaving you with a gift—peace of mind and heart. And the peace I give is a gift the world cannot give. So don't be troubled or afraid." These words of Jesus are found in the gospel of John, chapter 14, verse 27.

YOUR NEW LIFE

Once you are on the other side of your miracle, as part of the new life you now enjoy, take the time to give back to others. Listen more; hug more; start a support group; and give your time to the promotion of organ donation.

Tell Your Story

I have met many who think that what they have experienced—whether involving cancer, diabetes, arthritis, heart problems, etc.—is not worth sharing. One man insisted, "Oh, thousands of people have gone through medical emergencies. Nobody's really interested."

Please erase that thought. You will meet certain individuals who are placed in your path for a purpose. They need to hear your voice—what you have learned, the emotions you feel, and how it has affected you. Just one such encounter can have a ripple effect that will not just touch one life, but hundreds.

There are those who live for money, power, prestige, or the next promotion. They need to hear how your life has new values, and how a tragedy has affected your outlook for the better. Hopefully it will change theirs.

Personally, I see the world through new eyes, and have become a different person.

This book is an expression of my desire to share and not waste this tragedy that I have experienced. While I do not know how it will resonate in the lives of others, at the least I want to honor organ donors who have passed away and pay tribute to their families.

Don't Wish For The Life You Had

Of course, I would love to be healed and have none of the inconveniences that are part of my daily routine. There are so many amazing things that I used to take for granted which today I enjoy to the fullest. Sometimes even now as I take a deep breath I can feel a rattle or vibration in my lungs, depending on the date of my most recent bronchoscopy. Then I go through the checklist in my mind:

- Am I taking all my medications on schedule?
- Am I doing my breathing treatment?
- Am I faithfully going to rehab?
- Am I making healthy choices in my daily routine of eating and hygiene?

If I'm doing all I know to do, I will use what strength I have to help lighten the load for someone else.

A FRESH PERSPECTIVE

After returning to Charlotte, we needed a roof repair on our home. The estimator climbed up his ladder and surveyed the situation. When he came down, he said to Diane, "If it had been done properly when the house was built we wouldn't need to be here. And I hate to tell you this, but it's going to be expensive."

Reflecting on the year we had just been through, my wife asked him, "What are we talking about to get it fixed? A million dollars?"

The estimator laughed and responded, "Oh no. It's only going to be around two thousand."

Diane put the cost into perspective as she relayed a portion of my story to him.

FINISH THE RACE

Long ago, a man by the name of Paul the Apostle wrote these words: "Run with perseverance the course set before you."

In the final analysis, I believe that God allowed IPF into my life. As grueling as the journey has been at times, I feel like I have taken graduate level courses with my Maker, in my marriage, in my ministry, with family members, and a host of awesome individuals I would not have otherwise met.

While I wouldn't want to walk the same path again, in unexpected ways I am thankful.

Growth and maturity don't require life-threatening illnesses, but God gives each of us His strength for whatever we may encounter. I am grateful that He has given me a second breath to finish my course.

It is my prayer that in the low tides of life and unexpected tragedies you and others may face, these words have given you hope for today and the promise of a better tomorrow.

A FINAL WORD

As I write this, my health continues to improve. My stamina levels allow me to work part-time and return to a fairly active social schedule. I still have four stents in the airways of my lungs which catch microscopic particles and require trips to The Cleveland Clinic every 10 weeks for another bronchoscopy. The same doctor has performed every procedure except a couple and basically has my lungs memorized. It is important that we travel back to The Cleveland Clinic so they can keep on top of any abnormality before it develops into something serious.

I have been told that the lungs are the trickiest and the most risky transplant because they are a soft-tissue organ. Also, with every breath of the

20,000 breaths that an average person takes each day, I could inhale something that would trigger the beginnings of another crisis.

There have been no symptoms of chronic rejection setting in, for which I'm thankful. My doctors have always stated, "Our goal is for your health to become boring and predictable while you are living a vibrant and full life."

That is my goal, too!

One of the best parts of my day is when I can help increase the awareness or encourage a current patient with IPF. I've been given a platform and I want to be faithful in helping others as I was helped.

I am currently involved in donor awareness efforts and am honored to attend events that thank family members who have lost loved ones due to a tragedy. Even as they grieve, a circle of new life was made possible.

Every month, Diane and I co-facilitate "The Next Breath" support group in Charlotte with my lung mentor, David, and his wife.

Let me encourage you to visit the website of The Pulmonary Fibrosis Foundation of Chicago, Illinois— www.pulmonaryfibrosis.org.

The non-profit organization was founded in 2000

by brothers Albert Rose and Michael Rosenzweig, Ph.D, and is dedicated to identifying effective PF treatments and assisting those living with the condition. The brothers experienced firsthand the devastating effects of PF when their sister Claire passed away from this disease. Both brothers were also diagnosed with PF, and it was their vision and dedication that led to the creation of the Foundation. The site includes a nationwide directory of support groups, including ours.

In addition, we are privileged to be involved in ongoing fundraising efforts with The Cleveland Clinic to raise awareness and finances for ongoing research to find a cure for IPF.

The worldwide battle for dollars and donors is real. More research is necessary and needs to be pursued until a cure is found. Even as I write these words, more faces of friends that I have met who lost in their struggle with this disease come to my mind.

LIFE EXPECTATIONS

No one is absolutely certain how many men and women are affected by the disease. One recent study estimated that Idiopathic Pulmonary Fibrosis (or IPF, which is just one of more than 200 types of PF) affects 1 out of 200 adults over the age of 65 in the United States. That translates to more than 200,000 people living with IPF today. The statistics are sobering. Approximately 50,000 new cases are diagnosed in the U.S. each year and as many as 40,000 Americans die from IPF annually.

This leads to a question that many are hesitant to ask me personally, yet they really want to know: "How long does the average person live after a lung transplant?"

You will find a variety of answers depending on age and other factors, but most research states that more than 80 percent live at least one year after a transplant. The survival rate after five years is just over 50 percent.

To look at it another way, although a lung transplant may be a risky procedure, one fact cannot be ignored: 100 percent of those who receive a lung transplant would die without the operation.

Personally, I love to hear the stories of those who have lived 15, 20, and 25 years after their transplant. Recently, the Raleigh (NC) *News and Observer* newspaper featured the profile of Howell Graham, whose lungs were destroyed by cystic fibrosis. In 1990 he underwent a 14-hour surgery at the University of North Carolina Medical Center to replace both lungs. They were donated by a stranger—a motorcyclist killed in Florida.

Now, after 27 years, he enjoys life as a real estate appraiser in Wilmington, NC, and is the longest known double-lung transplant survivor in the U.S.

BEYOND TRAGEDY

As I have shared on these pages, life is filled with surprises and each of us has a story to tell. The good news is that we don't have to walk this road alone; there are people whose love and support help us make it through those darkest days.

As I look back, it is unfathomable to understand how intimately concerned our heavenly Father is with our lives. The God of the Universe, the same One who knows the number of hairs on our heads, is at work in every detail, and is orchestrating His story of faithful love to mankind—to you and to me.

Pain and suffering have tormented humanity throughout history. The world was not originally designed to be filled with tragedy. The painful reality that you or a loved one has experienced (or are still going through) may make the details of my story fall far short in comparison.

We are all human, and our setbacks can cause us to question how an all-powerful, loving God could accept and allow such suffering on a global and personal level. If that is where this book finds you, allow me to encourage you not to give up as you wrestle with these issues.

There are countless books, blogs, articles, and messages available that will help you find the answers you are looking for. Please don't stop asking, seeking, and knocking until you find true peace... which is ultimately found in the Prince of Peace— Jesus. His Spirit will provide the courage and inner strength you need to persevere.

You may be surprised by tragedy, but from personal experience I can tell you that the real surprise will be the faith, hope, and unexpected strength that will rise within you and lead to a brighter day.

To purchase more copies of this book or to learn more about the author and the disease go to www.surprisedbytragedy.com.

You can read Tim's latest blog or send him a note from this website, also.

Tim has availability as a motivational speaker promoting and educating about IPF, organ donation, or persevering through tragedy.

CPSIA information can be obtained
at www.ICGtesting.com
Printed in the USA
FSHW01n2156190918
52145FS